ALL IN

How
Obsessive
Leaders
Achieve
the
Extraordinary

ROBERT BRUCE SHAW

HarperCollins
LEADERSHIP

AN IMPRINT OF HARPERCOLLINS

Published by HarperCollins Leadership, an imprint of HarperCollins Focus LLC.

Any internet addresses, phone numbers, or company or product information printed in this book are offered as a resource and are not intended in any way to be or to imply an endorsement by HarperCollins Leadership, nor does HarperCollins Leadership vouch for the existence, content, or services of these sites, phone numbers, companies, or products beyond the life of this book.

ISBN 978-1-4002-1223-1 (eBook)

ISBN 978-1-4002-1220-0 (HC)

Library of Congress Control Number: 2019956821

Printed in the United States of America

20 21 22 23   LSC   10 9 8 7 6 5 4 3 2 1

CONTENTS

1

GOING ALL IN:

FORTUNE FAVORS THE OBSESSED

Good requires motivation.
Great requires obsession.

—M. Cobanli[1]

Try this. Go to relentless.com on your phone or computer. Now ask yourself why the homepage for Amazon is filling your screen. It may seem strange that "relentless" takes you to a website that sells everything from tea to televisions—until you delve into the history of the company. Amazon's founder, Jeff Bezos, is arguably the most influential business leader in America today. His firm has transformed the way we shop and has forced competitors, large and small, to adapt to the digital economy that Amazon helped create. Bezos also disrupted the technology industry through Amazon Web Services and is now pushing into areas such as logistics, advertising, media, and health care. It is a rare person who alters the competitive landscape of just one industry—but it is almost unheard of for someone to do so in several.[2]

Bezos started his company thinking that the internet, small at the time but growing at a dramatic rate, would enable people to shop in a new way. This seems obvious today when we buy goods with a single click and they appear outside our door in days, if not hours.[3] However, what we now take for granted was much less certain when Bezos founded Amazon.

The internet was initially an emergency communication tool for the military. It evolved into a platform for academic and scientific researchers to share information and findings. Bezos saw its commercial potential and analyzed start-up possibilities based on the best-selling mail-order businesses of the day—including books, music, videos, and computers. He decided that books offered the most upside because the web would allow him to offer a vast selection of titles from among the millions of books in print—using technology to allow customers to quickly find, review, and buy titles of interest.

These potential advantages were compelling because they couldn't be replicated by conventional bookstores, no matter how large. The largest bookstore stocked only 150,000 titles and couldn't match the search-and-review capabilities of the web. Bezos still thought what he called his "crazy idea" had only a 30 percent chance of success and told friends and family who invested with him that they would most likely lose their money. At the age of thirty, Bezos quit his high-paying job at a financial services firm in New York and took an entrepreneurial leap of faith. Driving across the country with his wife to their new home in Seattle, Bezos outlined his business plan and considered potential names for his new venture.

One that he liked was relentless.com, believing that good things came to those with the ability to focus intensely. This was certainly true in his own life. Bezos applied himself with a rigor that those who knew him viewed as exceptional. A story from his youth gives some insight into his personality. His Montessori teachers told his mother that her young son was unique in being completely engrossed in school activities. At times they had no choice but to pick up Jeff's chair, with Jeff still in it, to get him away from what he was doing and on to the next classroom activity. Childhood stories, when told by famous individuals and their parents, are prone to exaggeration. However, those who have worked with Bezos over the years describe him as being exceptionally intense and methodical in just about everything he does.[4]

Bezos registered the relentless.com domain name soon after arriving in Seattle.[5] He decided not to use it because friends pointed out that it was not a name that would help sell books. "Relentless" suggests someone or something that is single-minded, tenacious, and harsh. It is a word one might use to describe a wolf pack pursuing its prey. Bezos, after a false start with another company name, settled on Amazon. As the longest river in the world, it expressed his ambition to create the earth's biggest bookstore. But Bezos retained relentless.com and linked it to his Amazon website—perhaps thinking it would be useful in reminding his future colleagues what was needed for his crazy idea to become a reality.[6]

Over the next twenty-five years, Bezos built one of the fastest-growing firms in history. More than 200 million people visit its websites each month,[7] and it is the most trusted name in e-commerce.[8] Amazon's success, of course, is not simply the result of Bezos's relentless nature. Many relentless people don't build a successful firm, let alone one that can compare to Amazon. Bezos is a leader with the strategic ability to "see around corners"—noting patterns, trends, and possibilities that elude most people. He anticipated the potential of e-commerce when others thought the internet was little more than a research tool. He saw, despite resistance from his board of directors, that Amazon's technology platform would be useful to a wide variety of firms. He pushed the development of the Kindle e-reader and the Echo smart-device when few, if any, customers were asking for them. Amazon is now investing in a range of other innovative initiatives, such as drone technology for deliveries, to provide customers with products even faster and cheaper. Time and again, Bezos spotted opportunities that others missed and made long-term investments to capitalize on his insights.

Bezos is also operationally savvy. He has a deep understanding of the gritty details that are critical to his company's success. Bezos gets into the specifics of his business, how it is executing, and what is needed to enhance its performance moving forward. He knows, for instance, the intricacies of supply chain management and what is required to achieve ever-decreasing delivery times for customers. Watch him describe how Amazon manages its logical challenges and how the firm's fulfillment centers operate—including the intricacies of order-processing software and product-picking robots—and you might think he is a mid-level engineer responsible for operations management.

A colleague who worked with Bezos suggested, with only a hint of sarcasm, that others should view him as a super-intelligent alien—one requiring special handling particularly if you find yourself making a recommendation to him.[9] At Amazon, this often comes in the form of a short written proposal that is reviewed and then discussed by the firm's senior leadership team. When presenting, one of Bezos's former colleague recommends that others

> assume he already knows everything about it. Assume he knows more than you do about it. Even if you have ground-breaking original ideas in your material, just pretend it's old hat for him. Write your prose in the succinct, direct, no-explanations way that you would write for a world-leading expert on the material . . . tearing out whole paragraphs, or even pages, to make it interesting for him. He will fill in the gaps himself without missing a beat. And his brain will have less time to get annoyed with the slow pace of *your* brain.[10]

Bezos, however, is more than strategically and operationally smart—he is also lucky.[11] He describes this as "the planets aligning" to support his newly launched firm. Bezos at times calls his success and enormous wealth as him "winning the lottery." This phrase may be an attempt to appear humble in the eyes of the public but, even if so, Bezos seems to truly believe that luck was his partner in propelling Amazon forward.

He was fortunate in starting an e-commerce company when the internet was gaining widespread acceptance. At the time, it wasn't clear that the public would embrace shopping online, with many reluctant to order goods and provide credit card information to an unseen vendor. Comfort with the internet was on the upswing when Bezos founded Amazon, allowing his company to grow much faster. At the same time, starting Amazon a few years later would have resulted in losing his first-mover advantage over firms such as Barnes & Noble. Bezos was lucky again in some of his first hires, including a gifted technologist named Shel Kaphan who skillfully shaped the firm's all-important website. He was lucky again when J. K. Rowling published a block-buster novel, which Bezos used to build his customer base by pricing her book low and shipping it for free. But perhaps he was luckiest in having competitors who were arrogant and, even worse, slow to market. They made the mistake of underestimating the impact the web would have on book retailing—and also doubted that a small start-up in Seattle, whose leader had no retail and little business experience, could challenge their dominant industry position.

At the time, one of Barnes & Noble's founders said that, "No one is going to beat us at selling books—it just ain't gonna happen."[12] Barnes & Noble experimented with e-commerce by first partnering with America Online and then taking almost two years to launch an online site, which was poorly designed and even more poorly executed. The largest book retailer in America struggled to provide its e-commerce customers with the most basic services such as reliable order processing. Amazon had a window of opportunity to establish its brand and enhance its online capabilities.[13]

While recognizing that several factors must converge for a company to be successful, we can assume that Amazon would not have become Amazon if Bezos wasn't relentless and hadn't built a company with the same defining attribute. Leaders, particularly founders, imprint their personalities on their firms, which impacts performance—for better and sometimes worse, as we will see in the following chapters.[14] Bezos pushed Amazon, from day one, to embody the trait that had served him so well throughout his life. What separates successful entrepreneurs from inventors is the ability to build a team and then a firm that can commercialize their ambitious ideas. We tend to focus on individual leaders in explaining the success or failure of a company—and leaders such as Bezos are key figures in driving their firms forward. But success in business requires many people working together to produce something extraordinary. The relentless leader, then, needs an equally relentless organization to produce something significant. Read Bezos's annual shareholder letters and you find an innovative leader who thinks deeply about Amazon's culture and work practices. When asked which leader he most admired, Bezos pointed to Walt Disney, noting that

> it seemed to me that he had this incredible capability to create a vision that he could get a large number of people to share. Things that Disney invented, like Disneyland, the theme parks, they were such big visions that no single individual could ever pull them off, unlike a lot of the things that Edison worked on. Walt Disney really was able to get a big team of people working in a concerted direction.[15]

Brad Stone, author of *The Everything Store*, a well-regarded book on Amazon's history, observed that the company is built in Bezos's image—"an amplification machine meant to disseminate his ingenuity and drive across the greatest possible radius."[16] Amazon, then, is an institutional manifestation of Bezos's beliefs, values, and personality. Many terms can be used to describe Bezos and the firm he built, but relentless may be the most telling.

The second most visible business leader in America today is arguably Elon Musk. He is approaching cult status because he designs, builds, and markets one revolutionary product after another. The electric car industry was stagnant, at best, until Musk developed the Tesla S. The high-performance version of this vehicle received the highest rating ever awarded by Consumer Reports.[17] It also achieved the highest safety rating of any vehicle ever tested by the US regulatory agency NHTSA.[18] To date, Tesla has sold over six hundred thousand electric cars, which have traveled more than ten billion miles.[19] His vehicles have saved an estimated four million metric tons of CO_2 compared to internal combustion equivalents.[20] Musk also founded SpaceX, which became the first private company to launch a rocket to dock with the International Space Station. It was also the first to develop a reusable rocket—which has drastically reduced the cost of transporting materials and equipment, such as satellites, into space. What Musk has achieved is all the more remarkable because he is competing with well-established firms, such as BMW in automobiles and Boeing in aerospace. Bill Gates summarized Musk's achievements best when he said, "There's no shortage of people with a vision for the future. What makes Elon exceptional is his ability to make his come true."[21]

If we think of Jeff Bezos as relentless, it is equally appropriate to think of Elon Musk as obsessive. The word obsessive comes to us from the Middle Ages, when it described the siege of a town or castle by an invading army.[22] Over time the word evolved and took on a religious significance, referring to those haunted or possessed by an evil force. Several centuries later, the meaning of obsession changed yet again, this time to being viewed as a psychological disorder. An invading army became an invading spirit that became an invading thought. Most now see obsession as an overwhelming and unwanted fixation on a single idea, person, or thing. An example is an individual who is consumed by an irrational fear of germs—on a restaurant table, restroom door, or the hand of the person he or she just met. Their obsession can go beyond unwanted and recurring thoughts, resulting in compulsive behaviors such as washing one's hands thirty times a day. This type of obsessive-compulsive disorder, while sometimes viewed as curious or even funny, is a severe and debilitating disease that can torment a person.[23]

Some obsessions are less extreme but of debatable value. Marion Strokes was a librarian and civil rights activist who taped news shows nonstop for thirty-five years. At the time of her death, she had an estimated 140,000 videocassettes of TV news shows stockpiled in her apartment and various storage units—resulting in almost one million hours of recorded programming.[24] Strokes's motivation: she didn't trust the media and wanted to document how broadcasters filtered information and distorted the portrayal of various groups in society. She organized her life, and in many respects that of her family, around her taping. Every six hours she needed to insert new tapes in the numerous video machines throughout her apartment. Her TV archive may be unmatched in its sheer volume and duration. Time will tell if her tapes become a valuable resource to those wanting to research the history and behavior of the media.[25]

There is a third, very different, type of obsession.[26] An obsession can drive a person and his or her team to achieve something exceptional. An admirer of Elon Musk asked his former wife what advice she would give to those wanting to follow in the footsteps of successful entrepreneurs such as Musk. She said, "Be obsessed. Be obsessed, Be obsessed. . . . Follow your obsessions until a problem starts to emerge, a big meaty challenging problem that impacts as many people as possible, that you feel hellbent to solve or die trying."[27] These individuals, whose minds are "filled with one thought, one conception, one purpose" are those most likely to achieve something extraordinary.[28]

To illustrate this point, imagine you are leading a company that must choose between two equally talented and experienced individuals to lead a critical project. If successful, it will create major revenue opportunities for your firm and jobs for thousands of people. Making the project a success is all that matters to one of the candidates. She spends her twelve-hour workdays, as well as weekends, thinking about the product and how to best commercialize it. She has no social life outside of work and few, if any, outside interests. The love of her life is her work. The second candidate is involved in a wide variety of community activities and has a range of interests outside of her job. She works hard but makes a point to leave the office at 5:00 p.m. and rarely works over the weekend. Who, then, do you put in charge of the project?

Some would suggest that the first candidate, overly intense, is at risk of burning out not only herself but the members of her team. Promoting her would also send the wrong message to others in your company because it conflicts with the importance of work-life balance. However, doesn't her singular commitment to the project also increase the probability that it will be a success? You don't need, or necessarily want, a company full of obsessive people. You just need enough of them, particularly at critical points in a firm's history, to achieve something exceptional. And doesn't everyone ultimately gain as a result? As one psychologist noted, "When people with creative energy succeed in putting their obsessional personality traits to good use, everyone benefits."[29]

A vivid example of obsession's impact is evident in the building of the Brooklyn Bridge over 150 years ago.[30] One of the great engineering achievements of its time, the bridge spans the East River of New York, connecting Brooklyn and Manhattan. Washington Roebling was the chief engineer of the bridge after his father, the driving force behind the project, died during an on-site accident. The elder Roebling was working on the Brooklyn waterfront when an incoming barge crushed his foot. Two weeks later, he was dead from gangrene—leaving his thirty-two-year-old son to manage the massive undertaking. One year later, Washington Roebling suffered decompression sickness from working in the underwater foundations of the bridge's massive towers. From that point forward, he was unable to visit the bridge construction site. Instead, Roebling spent the next thirteen years, with the support of his wife Emily and a cadre of talented engineers, supervising construction from his home in Brooklyn. The great structure was completed in 1883 at a high cost to the Roebling family—the death of the father, a lifelong illness suffered by the son, and years of total immersion in the project by a husband and wife. The bridge has become a symbol of New York City's vitality and is used today by millions of people who daily cross it on foot, bike, car, and train. It stands as a testament to the never-ending commitment of one family.[31]

The life of Alison Hargreaves is another extreme example of obsession's price.[32] She was the first woman to summit Mount Everest alone without bottled oxygen or fixed ropes. Three months later, she was dead at the age of thirty-three—caught during a storm while descending the world's second-highest mountain, K2. Following her death, some criticized her for being so consumed with her quest that she forced her two young children to grow up without a mother. She said she loved her children and loved mountaineering—understanding the challenge of wanting both in her life but committed to keeping both.[33] In her last interview she said, "If you are given two options, take the harder one because you'll regret it if you don't."[34]

There may be no real choice for people like Alison Hargreaves. Jeff Bezos believes that obsession chooses the individual, versus the individual choosing the obsession.[35] Like the invading army noted above, obsession in its most extreme form occupies the individual, who can become captive to its demands. But those pursuing their obsession don't need to do so blindly—they can strive to act with an awareness of the potential cost to both themselves and those around them for pursuing their "white whale." Hargreaves was fully aware of the danger that she was facing. She, like all world-class climbers, embraced risk but managed it in a matter-of-fact and highly disciplined manner.[36] Hargreaves also understood that there was a real chance she would die in her mountaineering pursuits. She had seen too many of her fellow climbers suffer that fate to believe otherwise. However, she lived with the belief expressed in one of her favorite sayings: "It is better to have lived one day as a tiger than a thousand years as a sheep."[37]

While corporate life doesn't come close to Hargreaves's level of sacrifice, those who are all-in do suffer consequences. They may sacrifice their health due to long work hours and the stress of pursuing an audacious goal. They will see less of their families and have limited time for community and recreational activities. Even when they are with their spouse and children, they are constantly thinking about work. Elon Musk is a case in point, particularly as Tesla struggled to overcome its operational and financial challenges. A biographer of Musk said,

> This guy is committed on a level that is insane. He has no life on a lot of levels. He works all the time. He has burned through three marriages. He doesn't get enough time with his kids. He doesn't have anything like a normal existence. It's a sacrifice that no one else would be willing to make.[38]

It may seem absurd to sympathize with those who achieve success at the level of Bezos and Musk. We must recognize, however, that being obsessed is not always a comfortable or happy existence. As Musk noted, most of those who admire him would likely not want to be him if they spent only a few days living his life. In the business world obsessive leaders can experience a level of stress and scrutiny that would overwhelm most people. The public may respect these leaders for their achievements and wealth, but most don't appreciate the sacrifices that they make in pursuit of their ambitious goals. Many want to feel what it is like to be Elon Musk and live vicariously through his Twitter posts and product introductions. Living in his world full-time, however, is far less appealing once the cost becomes clear. As Musk said about his life, "The reality is great highs, terrible lows and unrelenting stress. Don't think people want to hear about the last two."[39]

Obsession is often feared, not only for the price it extracts from individuals and their families but because of the toll it can take on coworkers. Steve Jobs's obsession with creating great products is well known. He took a company that was months from bankruptcy and put it on a course to become one of the world's most valuable firms. Apple's 700 million customers and the 2.4 million people who work directly or indirectly for the company owe a great deal to Steve Jobs.[40] Despite his astonishing achievements, Jobs is a leader with a mixed legacy. He has many passionate admirers as well as a smaller but equally vocal group of detractors. The primary point of debate regarding his leadership is how Jobs treated those who worked for him. Jobs would threaten and demean those who failed to meet his lofty expectations. He was aggressive in extracting the best from his team members and those reporting to them—no one was spared if they produced a product that failed to meet his expectations. One of his colleagues described Jobs's approach as "management by character assassination." He recalled,

> His management style was to commit to the impossible and drive his staff, often cruelly, to produce results. He treated his employees with a mixture of fickle favoritism and blame. . . . Mostly he just looked at you and very directly said in a very loud and stern voice, "You are fucking up my company," or, "If we fail, it will be because of you."[41]

Jobs, as tough as he was on his team members, could be equally combative toward those in other groups within Apple. His obsessive drive resulted, at least at times, in an us-versus-them mentality within the company. He would regularly criticize those in other teams and belittle their efforts and results. The conflicts escalated, and divisions among the firm's groups became more pronounced. The result was an attempt by Jobs to oust the man he brought in to run the company. When Jobs demanded that Apple's board choose between CEO John Scully and himself, the board backed Scully. This resulted in Jobs, one of the most visionary leaders of the past century, leaving the firm he loved.

Many, including those who admire Jobs, suggest that the harsher sides of his leadership style were unnecessary. They believe that he could have achieved as much—if not more—with a more benevolent approach.[42] This view, however, ignores the reality that what drove Jobs to be an extraordinary leader, particularly in his unrelenting focus on designing great products, was the same trait that made him a tough boss and difficult colleague.[43] A leader passionate about creating something extraordinary is also a leader who can be hard on those who fail to measure up to his or her exacting standards. They have little or no patience for those who lack talent and stand in the way of achieving their vision. Jeff Bezos has at times received similar criticism, as has Elon Musk.[44] Many of the highest-growth, most innovative firms built over the past few decades—such as Apple, Amazon, Tesla, Netflix, Facebook, and Alibaba—were founded by obsessive leaders who demanded much of themselves and their colleagues.

Obsession thus presents a dilemma for leaders in what it can provide and take away. It also embodies a central tension in many organizations. Companies want people who are consumed with their work. Many firms also want to foster a work environment that supports a balanced life for colleagues, where work is but one element of a healthy existence. They are less tolerant of the dark side of obsessive behavior, including employee stress and burnout. But efforts to reduce the downsides of obsession, however well intentioned, always risk going too far by undermining what is needed to promote a company's growth. In other words, there are unintended consequences of putting comfort and balance before the need to produce something extraordinary. Jeff Bezos, recognizing this risk, doesn't want Amazon to be any less focused and relentless than the day it opened for business. To Bezos, companies risk taking on the feel of a country club, in part, because their success allows that to happen.

Jeff Bezos, Elon Musk, and Steve Jobs are similar in their all-consuming focus and relentless drive. The central theme of this book is that these two traits, focus and drive, are essential for those striving to achieve the extraordinary. The challenge, then, is to take what obsession offers while minimizing its very real downsides. The next chapter examines obsession in more detail, comparing it to the popular notion of grit. I suggest that obsession is grit pushed to the extreme, with both positive and negative consequences. In the chapters that follow, I provide three case studies in obsessive leadership—Jeff Bezos at Amazon, Elon Musk at Tesla, and Travis Kalanick at Uber. I describe the obsession of each leader and what we can learn from his experience. The final two chapters examine the choices facing individuals and organizations regarding obsession, highlighting the pros and cons of thinking and operating in such a manner. For individuals, the question is to follow an obsession or not—and then managing the consequences of their decision. For the organization, the question is what level of obsession is needed to compete effectively, particularly when one's company is either disrupting an industry or in the process of being disrupted by others.

To appreciate obsession's logic and limits, several caveats are important to recognize. First, *obsession is not the only factor needed to achieve something significant.* As noted above and in the next chapter, an obsessive individual who lacks the intellect and creativity needed to excel in his or her profession will rarely produce something exceptional. Malcolm Gladwell, the author of popular books such as *Blink*, suggests as much when he says he could play chess for one hundred years and never become a Grandmaster. However, Gladwell's argument is that talent, while essential, is overvalued. The key to success in most realms of life is a willingness to put in the focused effort needed to master one's profession and, in so doing, achieve an ambitious goal.

Second, *obsession is not always needed.* A company that operates in a relatively stable business environment can survive for years without a cadre of obsessive people. A professional workforce will suffice if a company is pursuing a strategy that is not at risk of being undermined by innovative and aggressive competitors. However, exceptional accomplishments, which Steve Jobs described as "putting a dent in the universe," are almost always the result of those with an obsessive temperament and a willingness to sacrifice a great deal in the pursuit of their goals.

Third, *obsession is not entirely understandable or manageable.* Obsession, by its nature, is surrendering to a calling that the individual, as well as others, may not fully understand or be able to control.[45] It may be that obsession is powerful, in large part, because it is unconscious. At its best, it is a productive fixation that provides the motivation needed to push forward and achieve at a level beyond what can be done by those who are only rational. The mystery is that we don't know why obsession arises in an individual or how long it will remain. The irrational element of obsession can result in misguided or even self-destructive acts. Elon Musk, for instance, has insulted members of the media and financial community when he thought they were obstructing what he needed to achieve. He responded to an analyst during an earnings call by refusing to answer questions about Tesla's capital requirements and customer-order backlog. He told the analyst that "boring bonehead questions are not cool." Instead, Musk engaged in a twenty-minute discussion with a retail investor who has a channel on YouTube. Musk ended that segment of the call by thanking the blogger for not asking boring questions. The reaction in the media and investing community after the call was overwhelmingly negative, with some suggesting that Musk didn't have the temperament to run a public company.

Fourth, *experiences in an individual's life do not inevitably result in a productively obsessive personality.* We don't know, for example, what events resulted in Bezos becoming obsessed with customers or why Musk spends his life creating products that he believes will benefit humankind. I don't believe in a direct connection between one's upbringing and the presence of leadership traits such as obsession, as much as some might like that to be true. The narrative fallacy is to look for cause-and-effect connections where they don't exist. Therefore, this book does not contain a detailed history of each leader's life, which can be found elsewhere in their biographies. I focus on their obsessive ideas and behavior, however formed.

Finally, *there is a risk of glorifying these leaders and their achievements, which can distort what we can learn from them.* We must realize, however, that the opposite temptation is equally problematic. Some view these leaders in an overly negative light when they stumble or become too powerful. Bezos, Musk, and Jobs deserve our attention because they are among the most successful and innovative business leaders of our generation. They were willing to take huge risks and to push ahead when the odds were against them. They created iconic products and built companies that changed the way we live and work. However, each has made significant mistakes, which to varying degrees hurt them and their companies. These are complicated leaders with towering strengths and, in some cases, debilitating weaknesses. They can act in surprising, contradictory, and inexplicable ways. It is best to view each as both exemplary and fallible. My intent is to explore the nature of their obsessions and their impact, allowing us to benefit from their ideas and experience.

TAKEAWAYS

- Organizations need obsessive leaders, at various levels, if they are to survive and grow in a highly competitive world. This is particularly true if they are striving to disrupt the status quo with a new product or service offering.
- All told, obsession is both necessary and potentially toxic. It needs to be embraced but handled with care by individuals and their organizations.

2 BEYOND GRIT:
ALL-CONSUMING FOCUS & RELENTLESS DRIVE

BEHIND EVERY GREAT ACHIEVEMENT IS A GREATER OBSESSION

Each year ESPN broadcasts the finals of the Scripps National Spelling Bee. In the competition, several hundred precocious kids are asked to spell obscure words that might as well be from a foreign language.[1] Under time pressure and in front of an auditorium filled with family, strangers, and glaring TV lights, contestants advance only if they correctly spell each word in successive rounds. One misspelling and they are out—the intellectual equivalent of sudden death. Angela Duckworth, a psychologist who teaches at the University of Pennsylvania and recipient of the MacArthur Fellowship award, viewed the spelling bee as a natural laboratory for her research on achievement. In particular, Duckworth wanted to identify what separates the very best spellers from the very good.

She found that the most successful contestants possessed more of what she called grit, a trait that resulted in a greater willingness to engage in the tough work of preparing for the competition and improving one's skills. As you might expect, her research also indicated that verbal intelligence played a role in predicting who was most likely to advance. However, intelligence was unrelated to the impact of grit—in other words, each contributed in unique ways to a contestant's performance. Duckworth concluded that grit explains why some people achieve more even when they are no more intellectually gifted than others.[2]

Over the past few years, grit has become a hot topic in the study of achievement. Over nineteen million people have watched Duckworth's TED talk, and her book is a best seller. Grit's proponents describe it as a combination of purpose and persistence in the pursuit of a long-term goal. Even though there is ongoing debate regarding grit's impact on achievement,[3] its proponents point to its role in fostering success in a variety of settings. They have documented grit's impact in situations ranging from West Point cadets striving to survive boot camp to corporate workers attempting to meet their monthly sales targets. Importantly, advocates also believe that education and training can enhance grit. They claim that each of us can become grittier over time and realize the benefits of doing so. Duckworth, in particular, highlights the vital role of parents and educators in building grittiness in children and students.[4]

Obsession, however, is more than grit—more ambitious in its goals, more singular in its focus, and more relentless in its drive. To describe leaders such as Jeff Bezos, Elon Musk, and Travis Kalanick as gritty is to miss the mark by at least half. Jeff Bezos has spent over twenty-five years challenging conventional approaches to retailing. In so doing he has created a company that has significantly raised the level of customer experience across all industries around the world. Elon Musk creates electrical and solar-based products that will prevent what he believes will be an environmental catastrophe. Travis Kalanick, the driving force behind Uber, was obsessed with creating better options for moving people and products from one point to another in cities around the world. Obsession is more than pursuing a long-term goal—it is the singular focus and unrelenting drive needed to achieve an audacious undertaking. For those striving to realize their outsized ambitions, grit is like bringing a knife to a gunfight.

Obsession differs from grit in another way. Angela Duckworth, based on her research and experience working in schools, believes that grit has no significant disadvantages. She writes,

> I don't have any data that suggests there are drawbacks to being extremely gritty. Indeed, at the very top of the Grit Scale, I typically find individuals who are tremendously successful and also satisfied with their lives. However . . . this doesn't mean we should entirely dismiss the possibility of "too much grit." . . . You can throw good money after bad on particular projects that will never make sense. . . . Still, I think these problems are mostly about lower-level goals that are in service of your high-level goals.[5]

More, then, is almost always better when it comes to grit. But more is often less when it comes to obsession. The cost can be one's physical and emotional health, personal and work relationships, and—in some situations—career advancement (as the obsessed can act in ways that undermine their success within a company or team). With the obsessed, caring too much about one thing can mean that other things are neglected or sacrificed in the pursuit of their singular goal. Justine Musk commented on what it is like to live and work with an obsessive individual like Elon, observing that it can be exciting if you want what he wants, but "what he has comes at a price, sometimes to Elon, sometimes to people close to him. But someone always pays."[6]

BEYOND GRIT	
Grit	**Obsession**
Purpose →	All-Consuming Focus
Persistence →	Relentless Drive
No Downsides →	Costly Downsides

ALL-CONSUMING FOCUS

Purpose, the first component of grit, is amplified in the obsessed—resulting in "the domination of one's thoughts and feelings by a persistent idea, image or desire."[7] Other aspects of life fade into the background, becoming peripheral and viewed as a lower priority or even a distraction from that which truly matters. This narrowing of focus is common to those seeking to rise to the top of their profession, perhaps most visibly in professional athletes. A trainer of world-class competitors notes,

> I have never met a great athlete, or an elite entrepreneur for that matter, who wasn't somewhat obsessive. The really great athletes, the one-percenters, are generally totally obsessed with what they are doing. They place a higher priority on their sport than they do on work, family, interpersonal relationships, and even on their own health. In actual fact, many athletes seem quite willing to sacrifice the very essence of life to achieve athletic greatness.[8]

He goes on to say that, while some elite athletes dominate their sport without being obsessed, they are the exceptions, not the norm. Success in a highly competitive endeavor demands the ability to narrow one's focus. Take, as an example, the life and career of Ichiro Suzuki. He is the Japanese baseball player who became one of the best to ever play the game.[9] He holds the single-season record for hits and has more total hits than any other player in history if we include his years playing in Japan and the US.[10] Ichiro methodically followed the daily routines he started as a young boy. Stretching, hitting, and fielding—every day, week, and month without exception, initially under the watchful eye of his father. He continued his routine for his entire playing career, which lasted for twenty-eight years. Suzuki organized his waking life around five-minute blocks of activity, with each having a role in enhancing his baseball performance. The journalist who profiled him stated that Suzuki has "methodically stripped away everything from his life, except baseball," suggesting that "he's made a $160 million fortune and can't enjoy it. He's earned his rest but can't take it. He's won his freedom but doesn't want it."[11]

David Foster Wallace, writing about the lives of professional athletes, suggests that excelling in a sport demands the "radical compression of attention."[12] The media, however, often portrays athletes as complete, well-balanced individuals with personal qualities that make them more likable to their fans. Wallace writes,

> Note the way "up close and personal" profiles of professional athletes strain so hard to find evidence of a rounded human life—outside interests and activities, values beyond the sport. We ignore what's obvious, that most of this straining is a farce. It's a farce because the realities of top-level athletics today require an early and total commitment to one area of excellence. An ascetic focus. A subsumption of almost all other features of human life to one's chosen talent and pursuit. A consent to live in a world that, like a child's world, is very small.[13]

Obsessive behavior, of course, is not limited to professional athletes. Comedian Jerry Seinfeld performs over one hundred stand-up routines each year. Now over sixty-five years old, he doesn't do it for financial reasons, since his net worth is an estimated $800 million. "I like money," he says, "but it's never been about the money."[14] Instead, Seinfeld spends the majority of his time writing jokes that work—which he shapes and reshapes to produce the most laughter. One of his peers commented that most comedians are lazy bastards, while Seinfeld is a dedicated craftsman. When at home, he goes to his office in New

York City, sits alone, and for hours on end reworks jokes on a yellow legal pad. In some cases he will spend years thinking about and modifying a single joke—altering its flow, inserting or deleting a word, and changing the way he delivers it in front of an audience. His life is one of fine-tuning jokes, smoothing things out, and making one small fix after another. He sees himself, above all, as a stand-up comedian whose purpose is to make people laugh, and the details matter. He then tests his improvements in stand-up appearances, sometimes to audiences of fewer than twenty people. He needs to perform the joke to determine if his changes are an improvement—or, as is often the case, realizing that further refinement is needed. In describing his existence, Seinfeld says, "A lot of the stuff I do is out of pure obsessiveness."[15]

A singular focus is also conspicuous in some business leaders. Nikola Tesla, the legendary inventor of the electrical and radio technology that impacts much of our daily lives, was such an individual. His contributions include the development of alternating current, which is the basis of power grids in use around the world today. He also pioneered the use of the induction motor found in a variety of devices and appliances. He wrote of what he valued most, "I do not think there is any thrill that can go through the human heart like that felt by the inventor as he sees some creation of the brain unfolding to success. . . . Such emotions make a man forget food, sleep, friends, love, everything."[16] Tesla's single-minded focus on his work came with a price—he neglected his health, relationships, and financial security. He died living alone in a hotel room in New York City, in poor health and financially destitute.

RELENTLESS DRIVE

Persistence, a key component of grit, becomes in the obsessed a relentless drive to achieve one's goal. Focus without drive means that ideas, even the most promising, may never result in a product or service that consumers value. Garrett Camp is the entrepreneur who created the phone app that allowed Uber to exist. But it was Travis Kalanick who had the unwavering drive needed to create the company that now serves fifteen million riders a day. Camp deliberately brought Kalanick into the firm because he had the ambition and tenacity required to overcome the daunting obstacles that Uber would face. Kalanick, not Camp, had the temperament to drive the growth of Uber.

Relentless drive operates at several levels. First, those who are relentless often set higher standards than others. To them, good is not good enough. Consider the practices of the legendary filmmaker Stanley Kubrick. For one of his films, Kubrick had a photographer take pictures of every building on a road in London that would be the site of an upcoming shoot. Kubrick needed the photos to ensure that the scene would be what he wanted. One of his crew members recalled,

> But crucially, he didn't want perspective to get in the way—if taken from street level, the buildings would look tilted backwards, and he wouldn't be able to line them up properly. . . . So the photographer had to take a large ladder to the Commercial Road, climb up 12 feet in the air, photograph the first building, then climb down, move the ladder along to the next building, and climb up to take the next photo. All along the road (it's not short). Both sides. All the while fielding phone calls from the director asking him to hurry up and how soon could he get the photos back to him.[17]

In the world of business, leaders can be equally relentless. In particular, some demand the highest performance from themselves and their colleagues. Steve Jobs, for example, wanted Apple computers to be elegantly designed—inside and out. Early in his career he observed that some of the components on the logic boards in the Apple II computer were misaligned. He made his team redo the boards, even though doing so would have no impact on the machine's performance and wouldn't be noticed by the vast majority of users (who would never open their tightly sealed computers to look inside).[18]

Jeff Bezos mandated that Amazon's e-reader be capable of downloading a book anywhere and anytime in less than sixty seconds. This meant the device needed to have internet access without being connected to a computer or Wi-Fi. We take the Kindle's ability for granted today. However, a tremendous amount of work was needed to make Bezos's vision a reality (including negotiating with phone companies to allow book downloads without charging buyers).

Elon Musk is another example of a leader who sets unreasonable, and at times unachievable, targets—pushing people to deliver more than they think possible. One of Musk's engineers at SpaceX said, "There were times when I thought he was off his rocker. . . . When I first met him [he said], 'How much do you think we can get the cost of an engine down, compared to what you were predicting they'd cost at TRW?' I said, 'Oh, probably a factor of three.' He said, 'We need a factor of 10.' I thought, 'That's kind of crazy.' But in the end, we're closer to his number!"[19]

Relentless leaders are also inclined to get involved in operational details. Most management experts maintain that senior executives should avoid micromanaging and instead delegate operational management to others. In contrast, obsessive leaders dive into the details and exert their will on how things are done. Elon Musk is actively involved in the design and manufacturing of SpaceX rockets. He is the CEO and chief technology officer of the firm. He said, "I know my rocket inside out and backward. I can tell you the heat-treating temper of the skin material, where it changes, why we chose that material, the welding technique . . . down to the gnat's ass."[20] Jobs paid attention to the smallest details of Apple's products and Bezos, particularly in the early years, would drill down to assess the operational minutiae of his company.

Another trait of the relentless is resourcefulness—an ability to find solutions to challenging problems. Bezos attributes his resourcefulness to the influence of his grandfather, who owned a twenty-five-thousand-acre ranch near San Antonio, Texas. From the ages of four to sixteen, Bezos spent each summer working with his grandfather. He wrote years later,

> Ranchers—and anybody I think who works in rural areas—they learn how to be very self-reliant, and whether they're farmers, whatever it is they're doing, they have to rely on themselves for a lot of things. My grandfather did sort of all of his own veterinary care on the cattle. We would, you know, repair the D-6 Caterpillar bulldozer when it broke, and it had gears this big, you know. We would build cranes to lift the gears out. This is just a very common sort of thing that folks in faraway places do.[21]

Bezos believed his grandfather could overcome any problem that he encountered, even if he had no experience with it. When rebuilding a tractor engine with him, both were learning in real time from manuals to guide their actions. Bezos expects the same type of resourcefulness of his colleagues at Amazon. For instance, he pushed the leader of an Amazon distribution center to allow customers to place an order as late as 7:00 p.m. and still get the product delivered the next day. The leader resisted but Bezos persisted—and the goal was met. Not surprisingly, Amazon goes to great lengths to hire those with a track record of being resourceful. The screening process at the firm includes extensive reference checks that include questions such as, "Can you think of a problem that everyone thought was unsolvable that this person solved?"

Being resourceful requires a willingness to push through the discomfort that comes with doing something difficult. This mind-set is closer to the historical meaning of the word passion, which is still evident in some countries today:

> In German, the word for passion is *Leidenschaft*, which literally means the ability to endure adversity. It is a much less rosy word, not the graduation bromide its English counterpart has become. If you're passionate about something in Germanic cultures, you don't necessarily enjoy it. *Leidenschaft* is about knowing the pursuit will be unpleasant but tolerating it because the outcome is worth the cost.[22]

Elon Musk personifies this harder definition of the word passion. His SpaceX Falcon rocket failed on its first three launches. A fourth failure would have likely resulted in the entire firm failing, since potential customers would come to doubt the firm's ability to launch rockets into orbit. Musk was asked how he remained optimistic after yet another launch failure and responded, "Optimism, pessimism, fuck that—we're going to make it happen. As God is my bloody witness, I'm hell-bent on making it work."[23] True to his word, the next Falcon launch was successful, and SpaceX landed a $1.6 billion contract from NASA.[24]

Research suggests that some persevere when others quit because they experience adversity differently. Carol Dweck, a professor at Stanford University, studies how people respond to difficult challenges. In her research she gives people, often children, problems to solve that vary in difficulty. She then seeks to understand why some people embrace hard problems while others don't. In other words, she wants to know why some push ahead to solve a challenging problem. Her findings indicate that how people interpret setbacks when solving problems is the key to predicting their behavior. Those who see them as solvable are more likely to push forward. They don't personalize setbacks or interpret them as a sign of shortcomings. These people have what Dweck calls a "growth mind-set," because they believe they will learn from every setback. This gives them the motivation and confidence to keep going when confronted with experiences that most people interpret as failures. In contrast, those who stopped working on a problem viewed their failures as the result of their deficiencies.[25] The ability to push through adversity depended primarily on how people viewed challenges and, in particular, setbacks.

OBSESSION'S COSTLY DOWNSIDES

As noted above, obsession is different than grit in the risks that come with it—which need to be monitored and managed. Several common pitfalls are especially crucial:

Personal Burnout

Obsessive individuals are always at risk of wearing themselves out physically, mentally, and emotionally. Those who are all-in may sacrifice their health, family, and social life in the pursuit of a goal. Their focus can become so singular that they view everything else as taking time away from that which they value the most. Elon Musk, reflecting on the personal price he pays for his work, noted, "Creating a company is almost like having a child. . . . So it's sort of like, how do you say your child should not have food?"[26] During a period of "production hell" at Tesla, he would sleep on the factory floor in his all-out effort to fix the problems on his manufacturing line. He said he wasn't doing it because he saw it as a fun experience—he was doing it because his "child" was in deep trouble. Musk worked even longer hours than usual—reportedly 120 hours a week for months on end. He said doing so came at a high cost to his health and family life.

Research into the nature of work engagement helps explain the potential downside of obsession. In one study, researchers found that three in five workers are highly engaged at work.[27] Most of those in this group experienced the positives of being so (intense interest in their work, desire to learn new skills, commitment to achieving a goal . . .).[28] However, some people in the highly engaged group, one out of five in the total sample, also reported a high level of stress and frustration. Their engagement had a downside that threatened to overwhelm the positives that came with being highly committed. To those in this situation, work was a grind that took a toll on their mental and physical well-being. The researchers called these individuals the "engaged-exhausted" group. They valued their work but were also more likely to look for another job, even more than those not engaged with their work. When looking at what caused the discomfort of the "engaged-exhausted" group, the researchers found that the key was the nature of the work itself—the challenges it presented and the stress it created. They concluded that the higher the work demands, the more people needed support and opportunities for recovery from the work itself.[29]

Individuals whose minds are "filled with one thought, one conception, one purpose"[30] can also experience problems in their relationships. One of the most famous studies conducted on the psychology of health tracked the long-term well-being of two large groups of men.[31] The primary conclusion of the studies was that physical and emotional health are powerfully influenced by good relationships. However, being consumed with one's work can easily take a toll on relationships with family members and friends.[32]

The leaders profiled in this book have encountered their share of problems, at least with their partners and spouses. Jobs was taken to court for child support by the mother of his first daughter. Musk has been divorced three times and Bezos's long-term marriage has ended. Kalanick has been in several relationships but has not married. These leaders, of course, are not unique, as an estimated 40–50 percent of all marriages in the US end in divorce.[33] The anecdotal evidence, however, suggests that being married to someone who is obsessed with his or her work can be challenging. After his most recent divorce, Elon Musk told an interviewer that he wanted to be in a relationship but wondered if he could do so because of the time he dedicates to his work and children. He asked the interviewer if he thought ten hours a week would be enough to make a relationship work.[34]

Ethical Breakdowns

Leaders with the greatest capacity to achieve the exceptional may also possess the greatest capacity to damage what they create. In some cases, this involves ethical shortcomings. Take the actions of Anthony Levandowski. He is a pioneer in the development of autonomous vehicles. His motivation was in part entrepreneurial, as billions of dollars in revenue would come to the first company to develop the technology. The other motivation was altruistic—as self-driving cars would be far safer than conventional cars and offer life-changing assistance, such as to the elderly and disabled.[35]

Levandowski's interest in autonomous vehicles started while he was in college, where his advisor described him as "probably the most creative undergraduate I've encountered in twenty years."[36] On being hired by Google, he played a key role in developing both what became Google Street View as well as an enhanced version of Google Maps. These products are used daily by millions of people. Levandowski then gained support within Google to focus on autonomous cars. Google's senior leadership viewed him as a creative thinker who was able to deliver on his wildly innovative ideas.

A journalist profiling his efforts noted, "His mad enthusiasm for the project was matched only by his technical grasp of its challenges—and his willingness to go to any lengths to meet them."[37] In particular,

Levandowski would push through obstacles, including Google's bureaucratic policies and practices, to achieve his goal. One example was his buying over one hundred cars needed for his research. Instead of going through formal approval channels, he bought the cars and then expensed them back to the company. The result was a personal expense report larger than all the other expense reports in his division—combined. Google's leadership reportedly tolerated some of Levandowski's more questionable behavior because they believed that he could make things happen when others could not. Some within the company believed that Google needed people like Levandowski if it was to generate significant new growth streams beyond advertising—which today accounts for the majority of its revenue.

The cost of supporting Levandowski soon became clear. Depending on one's point of view, he was either a highly productive leader doing what was needed to advance the development of autonomous cars, or an arrogant, self-serving and unprincipled opportunist. One of his coworkers said, "He was that type of guy. You know, an asshole. But a really gifted one. Our asshole, I guess."[38] Levandowski started negotiating with Google's competitors to sell technologies that he had developed outside of his Google role. He claimed that it was legal because Google did not have an agreement with him that restricted the use of his technology by other firms. Colleagues raised their concerns, but reports suggest that Google's senior leaders were insistent that the company retain Levandowski. Google bought Levandowski's companies and agreed to give him a percentage of the autonomous car's future value, which eventually resulted in a $120 million payment. But the goodwill created by these actions soon ended, as Google learned that Levandowski was planning to form a firm to build autonomous trucks and was recruiting Google employees to join him in the new venture. Google fired him.

Levandowski's newly established firm was bought by Uber, one of Google's primary competitors in developing autonomous cars. Google then sued Levandowski and Uber for stealing its intellectual property, charging that Levandowski illegally took proprietary files from Google's servers. Uber and Google eventually settled the case with a payout to Google but not before Uber fired Levandowski for failing to cooperate in handing over evidence requested by the court (and instead evoking his Fifth Amendment right to avoid doing so). There is a debate in the tech community on the severity of Levandowski's transgressions and why Google pursued him so aggressively in court. However, it is clear that Levandowski's obsession with winning the race to develop autonomous cars contributed both to his success and eventual downfall. Those who worked with him said he wanted to be rich, but his broader motivation was a passion for developing the new technology. He was a visionary with the ability to deliver what was needed—until he crossed what some saw as an ethical and perhaps legal boundary.

Punishing Behavior

For some leaders focused on achieving an audacious goal, the first and most important assessment of others is, "Can they help me achieve my goal?" Colleagues who can deliver what is needed are valued, while those who can't are marginalized, treated harshly, or fired. Long hours, excessive demands, and high standards can result in team member fatigue, dissatisfaction, and turnover. One long-term colleague of Steve Jobs at Apple noted that he felt at risk if he was anything less than "insanely great" in the eyes of the founder—stating that he and his fellow team members needed to prove themselves every day or Jobs would fire them. He added that, "It wasn't easy to work for him; it was sometimes unpleasant and always scary, but it drove many of us to do the finest work of our careers."[39] A well-known instance of Jobs being hard on those who failed to perform occurred when he met with the Apple team tasked to develop a file management service called

MobileMe. It was intended to allow users to connect and organize files in the cloud. The project was failing, and Jobs was furious. He told the group's members in an all-hands meeting that they had tarnished Apple's reputation and that "you should hate each other for having let each other down." He then fired the leader of the group and appointed a new leader on the spot.[40] His biographer, Walter Isaacson, noted that Jobs was extreme in his views—with a product or person being either great or awful. As a result, Isaacson said, in what some would suggest is a charitable statement, that Jobs could be "brittle, rather impatient, sometimes brusque."[41]

Jeff Bezos, as noted in the last chapter, is also hard on those who fail to meet his expectations. One business journal, profiling the rise of Amazon, published an article with the title "The genius, obsession and cruelty of Amazon's Jeff Bezos."[42] A publication headline isn't necessarily the truth but others, including current and former employees, indicate that Amazon can be a very tough place to work. Bezos, of course, sets the cultural tone and is known for having little patience for those who fail to perform at the highest level. A biographer wrote that Bezos has confronted those who disappoint him with statements such as, "This document was clearly written by the B team. Can someone get me the A team document? I don't want to waste my time with the B team document," "Does it surprise you that you don't know the answer to that question?" and "Are you lazy or just incompetent?"[43] One former employee said of his time at Amazon,

> I worked hard and had fun, but every day I honestly worried they might fire me in the morning. Sure, it was a kind of paranoia. But it was sort of healthy in a way. I kept my resume up to date, and I kept my skills up to date, and I never worried about saying something stupid and ruining my career. Because hey, they were most likely going to fire me in the morning.[44]

Bezos, like Jobs and Musk, makes no apologies for enforcing high standards. He also believes many of the criticisms of his firm's culture are inaccurate and unfair—that they portray a company that is much harsher than what he and his colleagues experience. He argues that Amazon is an intense but friendly culture. It is not right for everyone, and it is not a culture that every company should emulate. He says that it works well for those who want to pioneer and invent—and appreciate, as Bezos puts it, the need to work long, hard, and smart in pursuit of tough goals.[45]

Some view the behavior of these leaders as taking their obsessive drive too far. Others, however, suggest that their demanding approach is essential in creating innovative products that customers value. In his book *The Captain Class*, Sam Walker highlights research that distinguishes between punishing and instrumental aggression. Punishing aggression arises from a personal wish to hurt or demean others. Those who engage in this type of behavior are cruel for the sake of being cruel. Instrumental aggression, in contrast, arises from a desire to address gaps in performance—the difference between what exists and the ideal of what is possible. In this case, aggressive behavior is a means to a productive end and not a desire to hurt anyone for the sake of doing so. While we can only speculate, the behavior of the leaders profiled in this book is illustrative of the second type of aggression—exhibited in the service of a goal that ultimately benefits others. That may not make being on the receiving end of their aggression any easier—but it is at least understandable. In these cases, bad behavior arises from an unwillingness to settle for mediocrity.[46]

Consider two instances of leaders who have adopted what they believe are the benefits of instrumental aggression. Tristan O'Tierney, a Mac and iPhone software developer, said that he "sees the value in bluntly telling people their work is crap when that is the case. You don't make better products by saying everything is great."[47] Instead, O'Tierney challenges his people to perform at a level beyond what most organizations and leaders expect—and even what the individual believes he or she can achieve. Aaron Levie, another successful tech entrepreneur, tells his new hires that they have joined an organization that expects excellence—which he believes surprises many who are accustomed to lower standards. He says, "My lesson from Jobs is that I can push my employees further than they thought possible, and I won't rush any product out the door without it being perfect." He adds, "That approach comes with collateral damage on the people side."[48]

Bill Gates offered a warning to those who want to be like Steve Jobs, particularly in his approach to managing people.[49] Gates said that it is easy to emulate the less desirable aspects of Jobs's leadership style but it is more difficult, if not impossible, to replicate what he did uniquely well. Gates said that Jobs was the best leader he has ever seen in identifying and motivating talent. He said Jobs could cast spells over people to get them to work feverishly to achieve his vision. He warns that those who are less talented, and for Gates that meant everyone else, would only replicate the "bad" elements of Jobs's leadership approach if they attempted to emulate him.

There are leaders who cross a boundary that shouldn't be crossed—even when their motivation is to produce something exceptional. Linus Torvalds, the creator of the Linux operating system, was obsessed with developing the best operating system. The group, under his leadership, had a Code of Conflict to ensure that contributions by programmers were at the highest possible level:

> The Linux kernel development effort is a very personal process compared to "traditional" ways of developing software. Your code and ideas behind it will be carefully reviewed, often resulting in critique and criticism. The review will almost always require improvements to the code before it can be included in the kernel. Know that this happens because everyone involved wants to see the best possible solution for the overall success of Linux.[50]

The problem was that Torvalds went beyond being honest and humiliated those who failed to meet his expectations. Over several years, he sent hundreds of crude and demeaning email messages to those working for his firm. He wrote to one of his underperforming programmers, "Please just kill yourself now. The world will be a better place."[51] When his emails became public, Torvalds said he was proud of what he had created with Linux but not how he communicated with his colleagues. Still, he defended his behavior, at least in part, because it was one reason that Linux was so successful. He believes being brutally honest is a necessity that results in a better product. In other words, the cost of poor performance is too high to worry about being polite or politically correct. Torvalds recently admitted that he had gone too far and took a leave of absence as CEO. He is getting coaching on "how to behave differently and fix some issues in my tooling and workflow."[52] His group's Code of Conflict has become its Code of Conduct, with an emphasis on the importance of a safe work environment where members are "excellent" to each other.

Failure to Scale

Almost all significant achievements in business are the result of small groups of people working in a focused and collaborative manner. The need to be all-in, as noted in the last chapter, applies not only to the individual leader but also to his or her team. Obsessive individuals can, in some cases, lack the managerial and emotional skills needed to attract, motivate, and retain a high-performing team. As a result, they can't scale their obsession. Consider, for example, the boss who was fired because his obsessive style resulted in micromanaging his team as well as external vendors. He couldn't tolerate anything less than what he believed was necessary to produce a great product—and thus dictated to others what needed to be done. Negative feedback on his leadership approach, from both his team and vendors, was communicated to those he reported to in the company hierarchy. His supervisor told him that he needed to change his behavior since it was undermining the project's success. He was terminated after a series of conflicts with key members of his team that led his supervisor to conclude that he could not modify his approach. The irony is that he was the person most dedicated to producing something of high quality. The more he cared, the less effective he was because he could not work productively with those on his team. His style was even more of a problem in the collaborative culture of the firm in which he worked—one that values people working together in a team-based culture. It was also clear that he viewed himself as smarter than others and their shortcomings frustrated him. He felt he was surrounded by people who lacked the intelligence and commitment needed to achieve what he valued above all else. The result, however, was that he alienated those whose support he needed.

The leaders profiled in this book vary in their ability to scale their obsession. Jeff Bezos and Steve Jobs, although tough bosses, built highly talented teams of loyal colleagues. Elon Musk, in contrast, has experienced high turnover at Tesla and at times suffered because of weakness in areas such as manufacturing.[53] In contrast, Musk has built a strong team at SpaceX, which has become the dominant private space exploration firm in the world. The next several years will determine if he can do the same at Tesla. Another leader profiled in a later chapter, Travis Kalanick, was also challenged in scaling his obsession at Uber. At least at the corporate level, Uber had significant talent gaps in essential functions. His team drove the explosive growth of the company, but problems were either ignored or mismanaged by his leadership group. In addition, the senior ranks at Uber were decimated by resignations and firings in the years before Kalanick's resignation. His successor as CEO needed to build a leadership team almost from scratch because of Kalanick's failure to develop a robust team at the top of the company. Kalanick's fall from power was due to several causes, but he demonstrates that those who can't effectively scale their obsession will likely fail over the long term.

Tunnel Vision

An underlying cause of the pitfalls noted above is the tendency of obsessive individuals to have what cognitive psychologists call tunnel vision—which, in the cases of leaders, means they focus primarily, if not exclusively, on that which they believe is important in achieving their goal. Tunnel vision is risky because it focuses attention so tightly that other essential factors are ignored. Two professors working in the area of cognitive functioning, Eldar Shafir and Sendhil Mullainathan, argue that tunneling is especially prevalent in situations of scarcity, when people are without something they need.[54] Their research is based, in part, on the findings of a study conducted near the end of World War II on the effects of starvation. Europe was facing severe food shortages, and the researchers wanted to understand the impact of food deprivation and the best way to bring people back to health. To do so, they enlisted thirty-six conscientious objectors in an experiment at a Minnesota university. They put the volunteers on a semi-starvation diet for six months, on which they lost an average 25 percent of their body weight. The researchers noted that the participants increasingly thought about almost nothing but food. Everything else became secondary, as the body was deprived of that which it needed to survive. The researchers assumed the study participants would want to be distracted but found the opposite—thoughts of food filled their minds. They wrote,

> They basically were very hungry and couldn't stop thinking about eating. You know, in some sense, you'd think, given

that they cannot eat, they'd rather be distracted with other things. But in fact, . . . their choice of conversation largely was around food. Actually, it was sort of tragicomic. I mean, they planned to open restaurants, to become restaurateurs. They memorized recipes. They compared food prices of different newspapers. That's what they were doing. The whole time, they sat around looking at food-related issues.[55]

The professors argue that the tunnel vision apparent in those on a starvation diet also surfaces in other realms of life—when, for example, someone believes he or she has limited time to achieve a task. In the case of the leaders profiled in this book, the "shortage" mentality can apply to the time and talent needed to create exceptional products and services. Tunnel vision, of course, is not all bad. The ability to focus is beneficial when dealing with near-term challenges and demands. This results in what Shafir and Mullainathan call a "focus dividend."[56]

However, focusing requires the ability to de-focus from that which is viewed as being extraneous to one's goal. In that way, irrelevant or distracting information and demands don't consume valuable time and energy. "Focusing on one thing means neglecting another" because "the power of focus is also the power to shut things out."[57] Problems arise when one's focus is too narrow, resulting in failing to pay attention to other important factors. In these situations, the upside of focusing can easily turn into a downside. An example of tunneling, found in the book *Scarcity*, is the story of a firefighter who died in the line of duty. His death was not from what we might expect—fighting a fire. He died when he fell out of his truck on the way to fight a fire. He did so because he didn't put on his seat belt, and instead was concentrating on what he was about to encounter in entering a burning building. Paying attention to what he viewed as being of utmost importance resulted in him ignoring something also worthy of his attention.[58]

THE OBSESSIVE DILEMMA

Given the potential downsides of obsession, it is reasonable to ask why organizations and individuals don't simply aspire to be gritty. The most straightforward reason is that some challenges require more focus and drive than grit provides. Organizations benefit and, in some situations, even exploit an obsessive's "work-first" mentality. In return, obsessives get to work on that which matters most to them. If you want to decarbonize the environment through the development of mass-market electric vehicles, you can't do so by working in your garage and building a few cars. You need to work for a firm that is building hundreds of thousands of electric cars. If you are obsessed with space travel, you can launch small rockets on your own. But you are not going to reach the International Space Station or help colonize Mars. These individuals need to work in firms like Tesla and SpaceX if they are to do what they love. The obsessive individual and his or her organization are each using the other, ideally in a transparent manner, to get what they want.

It can be argued that there is no shortage of organizations that want obsessives in their ranks. They hire and reward those with the focus and drive that obsession provides. The reality, however, is more complicated. As suggested in the following chapters, obsessives can be highly disruptive and create a work environment that may not be sustainable over time. Some create unproductive conflicts and a level of stress that undermines an organization's or team's ability to perform at a high level over a sustained period.[59]

Consider what Musk's colleagues experienced as he pushed to increase production of Tesla's Model 3 sedan in the face of manufacturing difficulties and financial pressures. Think of what Tesla's shareholders experienced as Musk engaged in combative exchanges with the SEC regarding the legality of his Twitter posts. He is a technological genius who will act at times in impulsive and self-destructive ways that undermine his credibility and the viability of his firm. There is no Tesla, at least the size at which it currently operates, without Elon Musk. It is equally true that Tesla may fail going forward because of Elon Musk. He embodies the core dilemma facing obsessives and their organizations—obsessives are both necessary and potentially toxic.

The potential for good and bad in obsessive personalities can result in overly simplistic narratives about them. The positive story line is that these are people who have dedicated their lives to achieving a goal and who persevere in the face of adversity. The negative story line is that they have a win-at-all-costs mentality and can act in ways that are self-destructive and antisocial. Leaders often add to public distortions about them by striving to portray themselves in an agreeable manner—sometimes embellishing, or at least emphasizing, certain aspects of their personality when it serves their interests. Many leaders will repeat stories to influence how others view them. Jeff Bezos, for instance, often tells the story of how in the early years of Amazon he worked with his colleagues packing orders and delivering book shipments to the local post office. One of his first employees suggested something that hadn't occurred to Bezos:

> I said to one of the software engineers, who was packing alongside me, "You know what we should do? We should get knee pads." He looked at me like I was the dumbest guy he'd ever seen in his life and said, "Jeff, we should get packing tables." The next day I bought packing tables, and it doubled productivity.[60]

Bezos has carefully shaped Amazon's public image. But it is a mistake to view him, or others such as Steve Jobs and Elon Musk, as being primarily self-serving and narcissistic. Leadership obsession, at least in its most productive form, is an investment in something other than the self—often a product or service that benefits others. Obsessives generally don't care what people think about them unless it negatively impacts their company. Narcissists, in contrast, care a great deal what people think of them. Karen Swisher, a well-respected journalist who writes about technology, notes that Jeff Bezos can appear in public to be an easygoing leader, even one with a loud and distinctive laugh. She believes, in reality, that he is a tough and driven leader—one who doesn't care what people think about him. She writes, "A lot of tech people really want to be liked; Jeff is not like that."[61] We can assume that Bezos cares about how others view him only to the extent that it impacts their willingness to buy his firm's products and services—and more generally support his firm's place in society. The packing story noted above portrays a billionaire who is humble and self-deprecating. That makes Bezos and his company more likely to be embraced by the public. This, however, doesn't mean that Bezos wants praise for its own sake. Bezos goes even further and says that those pursuing innovative ideas need to be comfortable with being unpopular—in some cases, for years. This is because ideas that disrupt the status quo are often misunderstood or feared by those who benefit from the way things are currently being done.

While obsession is different than narcissism, the reality is that most great leaders have ample reserves of both positive and negative qualities. Nikola Tesla said as much when he noted that "our virtues and failings are inseparable, like force and matter."[62] Take the actions of Mark Zuckerberg in the creation of Facebook. While a student at Harvard, Zuckerberg worked with two fellow students to build a social media website. Unknown to his partners, Zuckerberg secretly developed a similar site that eventually became Facebook. There are conflicting explanations of why he did so. Some suggest that he needed to move fast to bring his idea to market and would benefit from operating independently. Others view his actions as being entirely self-serving. The lawsuit filed against him years later by his former partners charged that Zuckerberg stole their social networking idea and some of their software. A settlement was reached for reportedly $65 million—not a large amount of money for Facebook but enough to lead some to conclude that Zuckerberg was acting in more than an entrepreneurial manner.[63] However, we must also recognize that it was Zuckerberg who built Facebook into the preeminent social media company in the world—not his accusers.[64] His singular focus and relentless drive allowed him to build a remarkable company and also to act, at times, in ways that raised questions about his ethics.

Zuckerberg is not unique. At certain points in his career Bill Gates was known for being highly aggressive in pursuing what he wanted. Paul Allen, his Microsoft cofounder, worked closely with Gates from the time they were teenagers in Seattle. Allen said of his more famous partner, "You could tell three things about Bill Gates pretty quickly. He was really smart. He was really competitive; he wanted to show you how smart he was. And he was really, really persistent."[65] Years after founding the company with Gates, Allen learned that he had Hodgkin's lymphoma. After receiving medical treatment, he returned to work but was not operating at the same level as he had in the past. In his biography, Allen said that he overheard Gates and CEO Steve Ballmer discussing him, debating what to do given the decline in his productivity. Allen claimed they were debating ways to dilute his Microsoft ownership by issuing stock options to themselves and other shareholders. Enraged, Allen confronted them, saying, "This is unbelievable! It shows your true character, once and for all."[66] Ballmer and Gates apologized to Allen and said that they wouldn't have carried through on their plan. Allen, however, soon resigned from Microsoft.

Bill Gates is held in high esteem today, not only for his success at Microsoft but because of his global philanthropic efforts. He uses his wealth and talent to reduce poverty and disease around the world. If we take Allen at his word, Gates—who is fully committed to the betterment of humankind—is the same man who was willing to undermine his close friend and cofounder. This is not to demean Gates but to suggest that he is a more complex personality than his public persona would suggest. Like other leaders profiled in this book, he illustrates that those who achieve the extraordinary are rarely untarnished individuals. Their greatness comes with predictable flaws, particularly for those with an obsessive personality. Maximizing obsession requires that we both understand and value what it offers while also recognizing how it can go very wrong.

TAKEAWAYS

- Obsession is the all-consuming focus and relentless drive needed to achieve an audacious goal. It is grit taken to the extreme.
- Unlike grit, obsession has costly downsides to be monitored and managed.
- Realizing obsession's potential requires self-awareness and self-regulation—which can be in short supply as leaders relentlessly push to achieve their goals.
- Obsession also requires effective organizational responses, including skillful supervision and well-designed checks and balances.

PROFILES IN
OBSESSION

3 DELIGHTING CUSTOMERS:
JEFF BEZOS & AMAZON

The most important single thing is
to focus obsessively on the customer.
—Jeff Bezos[1]

One of the eye-opening facts about Amazon is that 92 percent of Americans who shop online have bought something from the company.[2] A customer, explaining its appeal, said, "We can either go to Amazon on our own, at 9 o'clock at night, and have [our order] there in two days. Or we could wait until the weekend, and get everybody in the car, go out shopping and hopefully, we find what we want."[3] Amazon gives customers what they want in a friction-free way—the "most convenient store on the planet."[4] It saves what to many is the most precious of commodities—time. One business expert believes Amazon is a natural monopoly not because of its size and reach but because of its ability to determine, at a level far superior to its competitors, what customers value and then consistently exceed their expectations.[5]

Amazon's ubiquitous presence in our lives makes it easy to forget that it was once a small and vulnerable start-up. Jeff Bezos was up against Barnes & Noble—then the dominant player in the book industry with hundreds of stores, thousands of employees, and nearly $2.5 billion in revenue.[6] Amazon, in contrast, had only $16 million in sales and 125 employees.[7] Barnes & Noble, however, was aware of its upstart Seattle competitor—Bezos was increasingly in the media spotlight and was soon to be gracing *TIME* magazine's cover as "Person of the Year."

Barnes & Noble wanted to strike a partnership with Amazon to sell books online, including a potential joint website. An Amazon board member, describing the meeting between the leaders of the two companies to discuss a potential deal, noted that Barnes & Noble's leader told Bezos that he could be a friend or an enemy. The board member commented afterward, "It was a pretty friendly dinner. Other than the threats."[8] Bezos, confident in his capabilities, rejected the proposed partnership and pushed ahead as an independent company. Barnes & Noble before long launched its website, with the intent of crushing Amazon. One analyst warned investors that Amazon's day of reckoning had finally arrived now that Barnes & Noble was focused on winning the online bookselling battle—suggesting that Amazon.com would soon become Amazon.toast.[9]

Bezos called together his employees and said that they had good reason to be nervous—but not about Barnes & Noble:

> We can't be thinking about how Barnes & Noble has so much more in the way of resources than we do. Yes, you should wake up every morning terrified with your sheets drenched in sweat, but not because you're afraid of our competitors. Be afraid of our customers, because those are the folks who have the money. Our competitors are never going to send us money.[10]

Bezos told employees that they could count on Amazon's customers, those who had embraced the company and the services it provided, to remain loyal—right up until someone else, be it a significant competitor or a small start-up, gave them more of what they wanted.[11] When asked about Barnes & Noble, he said that he was more concerned about a couple of unknown entrepreneurs working somewhere in a garage. Bezos told his people that they should not be distracted by the pronouncements of its larger competitor or the media profiles of Amazon—even when they were positive. They should instead keep their heads down and work to give customers ample reasons to stay with Amazon. He noted that innovative companies, by their very nature, are disruptive. This creates noise in the public arena, as people react to what the company is doing. Many analysts questioned Amazon's ability to grow without a retail footprint and, more importantly, its willingness to sacrifice near-term profits to invest in long-term growth. They believed its "no-profit" model would eventually fail. Others, focusing on the company's early success, believed that Amazon had a first-mover advantage. Bezos told his colleagues to ignore the various views about Amazon and stay relentlessly focused on customers.[12]

Bezos's colleagues did what he asked, and Amazon now has the highest customer satisfaction ratings of any online company. It reached $100 billion in sales faster than any firm in history and now accounts for 47 percent of all online sales in the United States.[13] In contrast, Barnes &Noble has struggled to remain viable in the wake of Amazon's ascent. One indicator of Amazon's dominance is its share price. One hundred dollars invested in the stock when it went public in 1997 was worth nearly $120,762 by 2018.[14] Barnes & Noble's share price over the same period suffered an almost 70 percent decline.[15] Amazon's unmatched success in online retailing and other industries has resulted in it being described as the "Death Star" that can disrupt any industry and threaten any company on which it sets its sights.[16]

From the beginning, Bezos was clear on the importance of being customer-obsessed.[17] He believes that no single business model is right for every company, and various approaches can work. He doesn't recommend that others blindly follow his firm's example; some companies focus on creating innovative products, others on leveraging new technologies, and still others on beating the competition. There are also those such as Starbucks whose ultimate purpose is to benefit society. Different models, if effectively executed, can lead to success. But Bezos believes that being customer-obsessed is the best model for Amazon. He suggests that "there are many advantages to a customer-centric approach, but here's the big one: customers are always beautifully, wonderfully dissatisfied, even when they report being happy and business is great. Even when they don't yet know it, customers want something better, and your desire to delight customers will drive you to invent on their behalf."[18]

He describes the "divine discontent" of the customer as guiding how Amazon operates. This is particularly important because it is easy to become overconfident and complacent once a firm achieves success or, in Amazon's case, reaches a dominant online leadership position. This can result in a company holding dangerous assumptions regarding customer loyalty, the correctness of its business model, and its "rights" to future market share. Bezos believes that the best way to avoid complacency is to be customer-centric. Since customers always want more, those who obsess over them are less likely to stagnate. Part of the problem is that yesterday's "wow" product or service quickly becomes today's "ordinary."[19] He wants to avoid the fate of Kodak, an industry leader that failed to capitalize on new opportunities and died a slow death. Being customer-centric is particularly crucial in fast-moving industries where there is a first-mover advantage for the most innovative companies. "If you're competitor-focused, you have to wait until there is a competitor doing something. Being customer-focused allows you to be more pioneering."[20] Bezos also believes that being customer-focused results in innovations that force competitors to play catch-up—meaning that they are consumed with keeping pace with Amazon (such as offering one- and two-day shipping) versus anticipating and staying ahead of their customers' needs. Bezos believes most large tech companies focus more on competitors than customers—regardless of what they may say to the media or public.

One example of Bezos's customer focus is when, early in Amazon's history, he emailed one thousand randomly selected customers and asked what they wanted to buy on Amazon other than books. He was surprised by the range of suggestions, which appeared almost random. Bezos concluded that the common thread running through the responses was that customers wanted to buy whatever they needed that day. He concluded those suggesting that Amazon should "stick to its knitting" (only selling books) were giving him terrible advice. Instead, Bezos developed what became the "everything store," one that now offers millions of distinct products.

The degree of Amazon's customer focus is evident in Bezos's annual shareholder letters.[21] A journalist analyzed twenty-three years of letters, which together contain approximately forty-four thousand words. He found the most-used keyword was "customer"—totaling 443 mentions over twenty-three years. In contrast, references to Amazon appeared 340 times, while "competition" appeared only 28 times. Bezos's emphasis on customers over competitors is clear to anyone who reads what he has written or listens to his speeches. It is not surprising that "Customer Obsession" is the first of Amazon's fourteen leadership principles.[22]

However, most large companies include some version of customer focus in statements about their corporate values. Walmart emphasizes "Service to the Customer," telling its employees to put customers first by anticipating and serving their wants and needs. What makes Amazon unique is taking the usual rhetoric about customers and making it come alive through a systematic approach to its business. The company has a well-articulated customer strategy and, more importantly, processes and practices that make customer obsession more than a corporate cliché.[23] Saying that your company is customer-centric is easy—doing it is much more difficult, costly, and risky. The question is, How has Amazon sustained customer obsession as it becomes an increasingly large and complex company?

BUILD A CUSTOMER-CENTRIC FLYWHEEL

Amazon's strategy is built on a growth flywheel. This is a strategic way of thinking based on the ideas of business consultant and author Jim Collins. The flywheel at Amazon starts with offering customers the most extensive selection of products at the lowest possible prices. When executed well, this results in a positive customer experience, which produces more web visits and sales from repeat and new customers. The expanding customer base attracts more outside sellers (to whom Amazon charges a fee as a percentage of sales). More paying customers and sellers provide the money needed to invest in upgrades to Amazon's infrastructure (including building new, highly automated fulfillment centers, more powerful computing capabilities, and the development of new product categories, such as the Echo smart-home device). These investments result in lower costs, faster delivery, and better products—benefits that collectively result in even more customers.[24]

Improvements in any part of the flywheel make it turn faster, resulting in a virtuous cycle that drives growth. Take Amazon's decision to give other companies access to the most valuable web real estate in the world. Bezos commented on the merits of doing so: "It was a very controversial decision internally at the time. Imagine being our digital camera buyer and you've just bought 10,000 units of a particular digital camera. Your boss says to you, 'Good news: You know all those people you've been thinking of as your competitors? We're going to invite them to put their digital cameras right next to yours on your detail page.'"[25]

Bezos, despite pushback from some of his team, made this change for two reasons. First, having third-party sellers would increase the number of products available to customers and pressure all sellers, including Amazon's in-house buyers, to keep prices low (since external sellers were required to offer the lowest price for their products on Amazon, in comparison to other sites and retail outlets). Second, third-party vendors allow Amazon to take advantage of its billion-dollar investments in an area, such as distribution, to earn revenue that will fund future growth. The sales of third-party products have grown at a phenomenal rate, topping 50 percent per year over the past decade. Amazon is now taking a similar approach with its logistics capabilities, providing shipping and billing services to firms that can't replicate what Amazon can offer.

The goal for other firms is not to mimic Amazon's strategy but instead to learn from its way of building competitive advantage. Each firm's flywheel will vary depending on its industry, history, capabilities, and customers. The takeaway from Amazon's experience is the need to be clear on the vital few areas that benefit customers and how those elements interact to accelerate growth. Amazon is perhaps the best example of how virtuous cycles can drive growth for those willing to invest in improving each area of their flywheel. Today, for instance, Amazon is investing hundreds of millions of dollars in building the capabilities needed to provide one-day delivery for most of its customers—which it believes will result in even greater growth for the firm.

THINK OUTSIDE-IN

An outside-in mind-set at Amazon begins with the customer and asks, "What decision should we make that is in their best interest and provides what is truly important to them?" This approach stands in contrast to what is common in many companies—a focus on defeating a competitor and maximizing near-term profits. When Barnes & Noble launched its website, it was thinking primarily of how to protect its core retail business from the growing threat posed by Amazon. Amazon was thinking about how to delight customers with new features and services, taking advantage of the internet as a powerful new technology. This type of thinking doesn't mean that a firm, including Amazon, is any less aggressive when it comes to competing in the marketplace. It does, however, suggest that the first consideration is working backward from the customer to determine what is needed moving forward. Bezos notes, "There's an old Warren Buffett story, that he has three boxes on his desk: in-box, out-box, and too hard. Whenever we're facing one of those too-hard problems, where we get into an infinite loop and can't decide what to do, we try to convert it into a straightforward problem by saying, 'Well, what's better for the consumer?'"[26]

At the next level of detail, Amazon wants new proposals to contain three elements. The first is a summary of the press release that would be used when launching the product or service, describing it and the reason it will appeal to customers. The second element is a "frequently asked questions" summary, anticipating what customers will want to know or the problems they will encounter with the product or service. The third set of documents portrays the customer interacting with the product, including mock-ups or screenshots of the customer experience. The specifics of each "working backward" approach will vary—the key is to start with the customer, listen to what he or she wants, invent a new product or service that delights, and then personalize it to the highest degree possible.[27]

Several services illustrate the use of outside-in thinking at Amazon. Just one year after going online, Amazon began providing customer reviews of books.[28] Many of the reviews were positive but some were negative (and a few very negative). Bezos believed that reviews would help customers determine what book they wanted and decided to publish both good and bad reviews. Amazon also averaged the customer ratings which were sorted from high to low (five stars, four stars . . .). While this seems natural today, when customer reviews of just about anything are available on the web, that was not true when Amazon started the practice. Some book publishers wanted Amazon to list only positive reviews—those that suggested the book was a good read and worth buying. One accused Bezos of failing to appreciate that he made money by promoting books, not panning them. Thinking outside-in, Bezos said that customers benefit by knowing what others think—which helps them make the best purchasing decision. Providing reviews would promote trust and result in more loyal and profitable customers over the long term.

Another example of thinking outside-in is evident in Amazon's decision to let customers know if they had already purchased a product. For example, people who buy a large number of books sometimes forget that they bought a title several months or even years earlier. They buy a book but never get around to reading it. Bezos decided that Amazon should provide customers with a warning that they may be ordering something they already own, even though it would result in selling fewer books. Bezos knew that customers would value a feature that stopped them from making a duplicate purchase. The feature would also prevent returns of books once the customer determined that he or she already owned it, which would result in an additional expense for the customer and Amazon in return shipping and restocking.

These two examples illustrate the customer-centric decisions that make life easier and better for consumers. The company, of course, does not obsess over customers for altruistic reasons but to build competitive advantage. Perhaps the best-known example of its relentless drive is the "One Click" checkout process that Amazon developed and then patented. All customer details, including shipping information and credit card data, are stored on the Amazon database and accessed with a single click when ordering a product. As with other features, we now take simplified ordering for granted in almost any e-commerce purchase. It was novel when introduced and became a competitive advantage. The firm's one-click patent became infamous for being unoriginal and potentially unfair (with some wondering how a company can patent such a general procedure). It forced competitors to add steps to their check-out process or pay Amazon a licensing fee if they offered "one-click" shopping. The story of "One Click" demonstrates that Amazon is tenacious in doing what was in the best interests of its customers—and itself.[29]

TRACK CUSTOMER METRICS—THE RIGHT ONES

Amazon backs up its customer-centric philosophy with a detailed set of customer metrics that Bezos and his leadership team regularly monitor. These metrics are much more pervasive and important than financial metrics. Bezos notes that standard metrics, such as net income and operating profit, don't appear anywhere in Amazon's 452 internal goals.[30] As a result, Amazon's approach to customer metrics is more rigorous than most corporations'; some lack customer metrics at all or use them in misleading ways. Customer metrics should be linked to a firm's strategic growth flywheel—which for Amazon, as noted above, means providing the best product selection, lowest prices, and fastest delivery. For instance, Amazon tracks the number of customer service calls per product sold, intending to reduce those calls as much as possible. Amazon views calls to customer service as a sign that it failed to provide what a customer needed—a sign that something didn't work. A call signals an error that needs to be understood and then prevented (versus merely addressing the immediate problem). Bezos notes,

> Our version of a perfect customer experience is one in which our customer doesn't want to talk to us. Every time a customer contacts us, we see it as a defect. I've been saying for many, many years, people should talk to their friends, not their merchants. And so we use all of our customer service information to find the root cause of any customer contact. What went wrong? Why did that person have to call? Why aren't they spending that time talking to their family instead of talking to us? How do we fix it?[31]

Of Amazon's hundreds of goals, almost 80 percent involve how well the firm is meeting customer needs, particularly in the three imperatives of selection, price, and delivery. For instance, the company tracks how long it takes for its web pages to load to a fraction of a second—it doesn't want people waiting to find the products they want. It also tracks product availability on millions of products, as well as shipping times on billions of orders. More complicated metrics include those such as revenue per customer click and revenue per page turn—"outcome" measures of how well Amazon is meeting its customers' needs.

Bezos expects his team to monitor and use metrics to improve how the company operates. In his book *The Everything Store*, Brad Stone described what happened to one executive who failed to do so. The individual was in charge of Amazon's service center. He was asked how long it was taking to answer the customer calls that came into the company. As much as Bezos wants to eliminate the calls, he also wants Amazon to do a good job of managing those that do come in. The executive told Bezos that the wait time was on average less than one minute. The problem was that his answer didn't include hard metrics to back up his claim. Bezos stopped the discussion and called the Amazon customer service number from the speakerphone on the conference table. In front of his leadership team, Bezos timed how long it took for his call to be answered. Almost five minutes passed before a service rep came onto the line. Bezos thanked the rep, ended the call, and harshly criticized the executive who didn't have the data to refute what the leadership team just witnessed.[32]

Bezos believes metrics, in most cases, provide data that allow a company to make better decisions. He gives as an example of the challenges facing his firm during the dot.com crash. Amazon lost over 90 percent of its value in less than two years. Bezos, however, noted that the firm's internal metrics were all positive. For example, the number of customers was increasing rapidly, and the number of order-processing defects was declining quickly. He told his people to stay focused on customers and building the Amazon brand. He ignored his critics, including those who said that he was only in business because Amazon was "selling dollar bills for 90 cents."[33] His metrics told him that the company would turn a profit and the stock would rebound as Amazon grew to a sufficient size, which, of course, proved to be an understatement.

RELENTLESSLY IMPROVE THE VITAL FEW

Bezos suggests that one key to a company's success is determining the few things that customers will always want over time—and then improving performance in those areas. During his public talks, Bezos is often asked what changes the future will bring. However, people rarely ask what will not change. In his mind, the second question is as important, if not more important, as the first. As noted earlier, Amazon's customers are focused on selection, price, and delivery. Bezos jokes that he can't imagine a time when customers tell him that they want less selection, more expensive products, and slower shipments. A primary role of senior leaders is ensuring exceptional execution against unchanging customer needs. He wants Amazon to improve before customers ask it to do so. This requires an internally driven improvement mind-set and attention to detail in the areas with the most impact on customers.

Bezos says, "I've never met what I think of as a good executive who does not choose certain highly leveraged activities—some area they consider so important that they will inspect it all the way down to the how stage."[34] The pricing of Amazon products is one such area. He understands the importance of pricing in sustaining a loyal customer base, wanting people to see that they are being offered low prices, if not the lowest possible prices, on the products they buy. He notes that he gets into the details of Amazon's pricing:

When it comes to the way we relentlessly drive down our consumer-facing pricing, I still continually launder and inspect that and talk to the people who do the work all the way through that whole chain. I need to be sure that we are in fact competitive and focused on offering our customers the lowest possible prices. That's one of the things I think is so highly leveraged that I am involved from heading level one all the way to heading level five.[35]

Amazon also invests in what is needed to make the company more efficient and, as a result, able to keep prices low. Take the improvements made in Amazon's large fulfillment centers, some of which are the size of twenty football fields. During the holiday season, the largest of these centers ship over one million packages a day. The company is now operating its eighth generation of centers, with each being better than the last.[36]

The firm's improvement efforts are often less grand in scope. Bezos regularly reviews emails from customers and, when appropriate, forwards messages to members of his team. The expectation is that a problem will be fixed in a manner that gets at the root cause of the defect (to avoid it occurring again for any customer). One of his executives said about complaints, "We research each of them because they tell us something about our processes. It's an audit that is done for us by our customers. We treat them as precious sources of information."[37] One customer noted that she had problems opening the packaging. Amazon then modified its packaging to make it easier to open.

The company sorts problems by severity, indicating the urgency of finding a solution. A problem with the web page loading would be an example of a severe emergency ("Sev-1" in Amazon jargon), requiring all necessary resources to resolve. A less important problem is rated "Sev-5." An email from Bezos is a separate category—which some unofficially refer to as a "Sev-B." Bezos will sometimes forward an email with a simple "?" notation—meaning that he wants the person receiving it to determine how the problem arose, what is required to fix it, and quickly get back to Bezos with the answer.[38] One of Amazon's leadership principles emphasizes the importance of what Bezos calls "deep dives." It states that, "Leaders operate at all levels, stay connected to the details, audit frequently, and are skeptical when metrics and anecdote differ. No task is beneath them."[39]

DON'T JUST LISTEN TO CUSTOMERS—INVENT FOR THEM

Bezos notes that many of the firm's most successful ventures were built by listening to what customers want and then providing it. He said of Amazon's Web Services (AWS) group,

> 90 to 95 percent of what we build in AWS is driven by what customers tell us they want. A good example is our new database engine, Amazon Aurora. Customers have been frustrated by the proprietary nature, high cost, and licensing terms of traditional, commercial-grade database providers. And while many companies have started moving toward more open engines like MySQL and Postgres, they often struggle to get the performance they need. Customers asked us if we could eliminate that inconvenient trade-off, and that's why we built Aurora. It has commercial-grade durability and availability, is fully compatible with MySQL, has up to 5 times better performance than the typical MySQL implementation, but is 1/10th the price of the traditional, commercial-grade database engines.[40]

According to Bezos, listening to customers is only part of what is needed to build a successful company. The other, perhaps even more complicated, task is to invent new products and services on the customer's behalf. He tells his colleagues that it is not the customers' job to create something they don't know they need. That's Amazon's job. One example is Amazon's Prime service, which offers unlimited shipping for an annual fee. Bezos likes to say that customers didn't know they wanted Prime until Amazon offered it. Over 100 million people are now enrolled in the program, which is one out of every two US households. Prime is also an example of experimenting with a new approach and then making it better every year. For instance, Prime now includes a range of benefits beyond shipping, such as streaming movies and TV shows. The goal is to have so many value-adding features that people feel irresponsible if they don't become Prime members. The Prime story is similar to what we are now seeing with Amazon's Echo device, which is not something that customers asked for but many now find invaluable.

Some of what Amazon does to invent for customers requires taking huge risks. One example is the feature called Search Inside the Book. Amazon decided that allowing customers to read a small sample of a book would be helpful. However, getting permission from publishers to do so was not easy. Scanning books was also an expensive and time-consuming undertaking. Amazon went ahead and initially offered samples from 120,000 books, which required a significant database upgrade to accommodate the new feature. Bezos and his team were guided by the idea that it was better for the customer and needed to be done. The same risk-taking was evident in offering Prime. Shipping is expensive and internal analysis conducted by Amazon suggested that the service would result in significant losses. Bezos knew that customers would love unlimited shipping with no purchase threshold—and went ahead with the program. It is now central to how Amazon engages its customers.

Another example of Amazon's inventing on behalf of its customer is its Kindle reader. Bezos saw how quickly the public embraced Apple's iPod to stream music—and in so doing decimated the sales of music

CDs (including those offered on Amazon). He knew that many firms had failed because they would not cannibalize their own business and, as a result, failed when a new technology eroded their business model. That's the Kodak story. As much as he focused on providing the customer with something better, Bezos was also afraid that another firm would develop an electronic reader that would undermine Amazon's market dominance in online bookselling. Bezos pushed ahead with the Kindle, despite Amazon having no experience building complicated devices. Some of his senior executives believed that Amazon would spend a great deal of money and still fail to produce something that customers wanted. One of Amazon's operating principles is to disagree when necessary, but then fully commit once a decision is made (even if it is different than what one believes is right). One team member wrote,

> When we were deciding whether to do Kindle, Jeff (Bezos) presented his idea to the board. I thought at the time, "We're a software company that built a retail business. We don't know anything about hardware." I'd come from companies that built hardware, so I knew how complicated it was. I said, "I don't think we should do this." I predicted that yields would be hard, that we might miss our first launch date, etc. Many of the things I predicted ultimately happened. But it didn't matter. Jeff at the time said, "It's the right thing to do for customers." I disagreed and committed, and I'm very glad I did.[41]

INCREASE SHOTS ON GOAL

Bezos believes in funding a large number of development projects with an understanding that a few will yield huge returns but many more will fail. The wins, when they occur, justify the many failures. Moreover, the failures produce learning that will benefit the company in its future projects. Observers of the company describe this approach as "Ready, Fire, Steer" versus "Ready, Aim, Fire"[42]—which is a way of describing Bezos's belief that it is acceptable and even inevitable to make mistakes—but it is unacceptable to be timid and fail to seize new opportunities. Bezos wants Amazon to support experiments at an uncommonly high rate—and to do so in areas that are not within the firm's current business model. It recently began to venture into the health-care industry, with the idea of using its core capabilities to provide people with better and cheaper medical products and services.

Pursuing this approach, Amazon has suffered some significant failures. It launched an eBay-like site called Auctions and then something similar called zShops. They both failed and the company killed them. However, they provided learning that resulted in what is now the widely successful Marketplace, where Amazon sells products produced by third parties. Bezos writes,

> That episode is actually one of the highlights of our corporate history—one that I tell over and over internally because it speaks to persistence and relentlessness. The basic thought was: Look, we have this website where we sell things, and we want to have vast selection. One of the ways to get vast selection is to invite other sellers, third parties, onto our website to participate alongside us and make it into a win-win situation. So, we did auctions, but we didn't like the results. Next, we created zShops, which was fixed-price selling but still parked those third parties in separate parts of the store. . . . We still didn't like the results we got. It was when we went to the single-detail-page model that our third-party business really took off.[43]

The success of Marketplace is still a work in progress, as Amazon works to provide necessary controls over third-party products that are illegal, mislabeled, or counterfeit. The Marketplace model has generated tremendous revenue for the firm, but presents challenges given the sheer number of vendors providing products to Amazon's customers.

Amazon's most visible failure is the Fire Phone—which lasted less than two years in the marketplace, cost the company $170 million in write-downs, and was widely panned by the media and public. It tarnished, if only temporarily, the Amazon brand. However, some of what Amazon learned through the Fire Phone, and the capabilities it developed in that failed effort, were instrumental in the success of its voice-activated home device, the Echo. Bezos believes that innovation requires a high tolerance for failure, which is inevitable when trying new things, calling failure the "inseparable twin" of invention.[44]

Part of Bezos's role as CEO is to say yes when most leaders would say no to an innovative idea. He wants Amazon to be an "innovation machine," increasing its number of experiments that are tested with customers to see what works and what doesn't. For every success story such as Marketplace, there are also many failures, large and small, that don't lead to new features and services.[45] For instance, Amazon experimented with matching a customer's buying patterns to others who bought similar items. The service went even further and matched the purchases of a customer to another person whose purchasing history was the most similar. This would allow someone to see what their doppelganger bought, suggesting additional items that they might want to purchase. Bezos said that what he and his colleagues viewed as a beneficial feature was ignored by customers, who didn't see any value in it and didn't use it.[46]

EMBRACE A DAY 1 CULTURE

Bezos uses the term "Day 1" to describe the culture he wants at Amazon. This was the mind-set of those who worked in the company as a start-up over twenty-five years ago. Companies frequently decline with age because they lose the energy and boldness that powered their growth in their early years. He doesn't want Amazon's phenomenal success to lead to an insular and complacent culture. Bezos has tried to maintain the spirit of a small start-up as Amazon has grown to be the second largest private employer in the United States with more than 650,000 employees.[47] The alternative results in the eventual death of the company because "Day 2 is stasis."[48]

Bezos tells his colleagues that Amazon, like all companies, will eventually fail. Their goal is to postpone that day for as long as possible by obsessively focusing on customers. Doing so can help prevent a company from becoming insular and risk-averse, particularly as it grows larger and more complex. Amazon began as a small start-up with no existing systems or processes. Everyone worked closely to sell and deliver books in an entirely new way via the internet. A deep focus on the customer was imprinted into the company's DNA. A Day 1 environment is familiar in a small start-up—but it is rare in a company that has grown to the size of Amazon. Bezos knows the challenge is sustaining the unique culture that drove its explosive growth.

The Day 1 culture at Amazon embraces a strong work ethic. At an Amazon town hall meeting, an employee asked Bezos about the demanding nature of the work environment. He responded, "The reason we are here is to get stuff done, that is the top priority. . . . That is the DNA of Amazon. If you can't excel and put everything into it, this might not be the place for you."[49] The demanding work environment has led some people to describe it as harsh. Bezos disagrees and notes, "Intensity is important. I always tell people that our culture is friendly and intense, but if push comes to shove, we'll settle for intense."[50] That includes, at least according to some employees, viewing work as the first priority. One noted that some in the company are fond of saying that "work-life balance is for people who do not like their work."[51] Amazon strives to attract "missionaries" who are likely to invent on behalf of customers, and will thrive in a customer-obsessed culture. Those who don't will feel out of place and leave. Bezos believes that, by this process, the culture is self-reinforcing.

Amazon also builds customer focus into its hiring practices. The firm wants to hire those who are more focused on customers than competitors (or short-term financial results). One of Bezos's senior leaders noted,

> In an interview situation, we use the leadership principles as a guide to help us evaluate whether somebody would fit in. There are lots of situations where you could decide to optimize for the customer or to get ahead of the competitor. We want to pay attention to competitors, but we obsess over customers. If I detect that they are too focused on competitors, they probably aren't going to be a great fit.[52]

The company uses employees whom it calls "bar raisers" to increase its success rate in hiring people who are highly capable but also a good fit to Amazon's culture. These are employees who have demonstrated an ability to assess potential hires, including the depth of their customer focus. They interview potential hires outside of their area of expertise with the intent of increasing the "hit rate" on new hires. They have the right to reject a potential hire even if the hiring manager wants to move ahead. The interviewing team needs to be unanimous before an offer is extended to a new applicant. Bezos would rather interview fifty people and not make a hire than to hire the wrong person.[53]

Bezos also notes in his 2016 letter to shareholders the importance of "high-velocity decision making" in a Day 1 culture.[54] He argues that Day 2 companies make decisions slowly, even when those decisions are correct. In contrast, a vital culture requires high-quality decisions to be made quickly because advantages accrue to those who move fast. This, however, doesn't mean that all decisions are equal. Some are what he calls an irreversible one-way door, and these take a more time-consuming and rigorous process.[55] However, most decisions can be made with less than perfect information, perhaps 70 percent of what a leader or team might desire. The key is to quickly correct wrong decisions, which minimizes potential damage and gives people the confidence to move forward decisively in other areas. This is in contrast to firms where people don't express disagreements, at least not in meetings, or don't commit to following through on decisions. Both behaviors waste time and undermine a firm's overall performance. The other key to operating effectively is to surface areas of misalignment as quickly as possible to more senior-level leaders to obtain a quick resolution. Bezos uses the decision to allow third-party sellers to list on Amazon's primary product pages as an example of the potential for misalignment. That decision was controversial within Amazon, resisted by some below the senior team, and resulted in operational gaps that needed quick resolution through escalation.

CUSTOMER-CENTRIC WATCH-OUTS

Customer obsession is not without downsides. A general concern for a firm that claims to be customer-obsessed is failing to deliver on the expectations it creates in the marketplace. As Bezos notes, what customers once viewed as remarkable quickly becomes ordinary (such as two-day delivery). Companies can become victims of their success if they don't fulfill the expectations they have created. A related general risk is a leader failing to be consistent in what he or she says or does. For instance, Bezos emphasizes focusing on customers over competitors and over time has reinforced this message. However, one of his shareholder letters described how Amazon had performed in comparison to eBay in growing third-party sales.[56] Why Bezos made this highly public comparison is surprising, given his past insistence of focusing on customers more than competitors. Amazon is, of course, aware of its competitors but has rarely strayed from its message that the customer comes before competitors. Other customer-centric pitfalls include the following:

Reacting Over Inventing: Firms striving to delight customers can settle for incremental improvements that respond to current needs. These firms may be responsive but not necessarily inventive. As noted earlier, customers typically can't envision radically new products and services. Bezos likes to note that not one customer asked for what became Amazon Prime. Customer obsession, then, needs to be paired with creative invention and a willingness to invest long term in innovative products and services. To his credit, Bezos has ignored critics, and even some of his colleagues and board members, to invest in innovations such as the Kindle and Amazon Web Services. The watch-out for those obsessed with customers is not to be limited by meeting only their immediate needs—both sides of customer obsession, responding and inventing, need to be valued and pursued. Amazon is an example of a firm that both listens to customers and gives them what they don't know they needed.

Proxies Over Reality: Amazon is data driven—perhaps one of the most disciplined in the world in the development and use of metrics to manage a company. Bezos loves numbers, as suggested by the fact that in sixth grade he developed a survey to assess the performance of his teachers.[57] But he is also suspicious of what he values. Processes, including metrics, can become more important than the outcomes that they are designed to achieve. Even when used with the best of intentions, metrics can become a substitute, or even an excuse, for not achieving customer delight. In his first shareholder letter in 1997, Bezos noted,

> Good process serves you so you can serve customers. But if you're not watchful, the process can become the thing. This can happen very easily in large organizations. The process becomes the proxy for the result you want. You stop looking at outcomes and just make sure you're doing the process right. . . . It's always worth asking, do we own the process or does the process own us?[58]

One way of avoiding this trap is to pay attention to customer anecdotes. A customer might say, for instance, that some packages are not delivered even though the metric suggests otherwise. It turns out that the driver was leaving them by the side door, which the customer didn't check. Bezos, data-driven and highly analytical, believes that anecdotes are often right when they conflict with the data. The problem often turns out to be that the measure is flawed and not truly reflecting the customers' experience. Amazon, to its credit, embraces but doesn't fully trust the metrics it uses to run its business.

Customers Over Colleagues: Obsessing over customers, if taken to the extreme, can mean that leaders view their colleagues as a means to an end. Those who are customer-centric can, at times, make demands of their people that are unreasonable and excessive. Moreover, those who fall short of the firm's high standards may be treated harshly. Amazon and Bezos have faced criticism for what some describe as a bruising corporate culture. Perhaps the best-known incident occurred in one of its fulfillment centers when employees suffered heatstroke during an exceptionally warm day. The site didn't have air-conditioning, apparently to save money, and, as a result, keep prices low.[59] Amazon's initial response was to have ambulances available in the center's parking lot. Subsequently, Amazon installed air conditioners in its fulfillment centers. An obsession, customer-focused or otherwise, always runs the risk of treating colleagues with less consideration and respect than they deserve.

THE GREATEST BUSINESS LEADER OF OUR GENERATION?

Few if any executives over the past two decades can equal Jeff Bezos's achievements. That said, Bezos is open about his mistakes, with the most visible being the Fire Phone. But there are other failures—including Amazon Restaurants in food delivery, Destinations in travel services, and Amazon Local in finding hometown deals. In his 2018 shareholder letter, Bezos noted that Amazon will likely make multibillion-dollar mistakes in the future, given the risks that come with being innovative. He believes that mistakes need to scale with the business—and expects the future missteps to be larger and more costly as Amazon continues to grow. Otherwise, the company is not placing the big bets that are needed for the firm to survive.[60]

The firm has also made political mistakes, as when Amazon misread the challenges of establishing a headquarters in New York City. Resistance to Amazon from some in the public and political arena resulted in Amazon pulling out of the project. Other missteps are personal, as when texts Bezos sent to his romantic partner were revealed in the press. Some questioned how one of the most sophisticated technology leaders in the world could assume that his electronic correspondence would remain private. To his credit, Bezos was transparent about the situation and publicly challenged the media company that published his communications when it threatened to do the same with what it claimed were embarrassing photographs. After the missteps of 2019, Bezos conducted an internal town hall meeting with Amazon colleagues. He asked those in the audience who had a better start to the year than himself to raise their hand. Almost everyone did so but Bezos noticed a few people who didn't, and, in a self-deprecating manner, said, "I feel sorry for you."[61]

Bezos's desire for Amazon to be a force for good in society is increasingly being challenged by some in the media, government, and public. More than in the past, there are attacks on Amazon's influence and power, resulting in calls to regulate and even break up the firm. Amazon is at risk of becoming distracted by the criticisms of its business model and practices, as happened at Microsoft in the late 1990s when it faced antitrust litigation. Bezos will likely do what he did when Barnes & Noble threatened his company's existence several decades ago—tell his people to keep obsessing over customers as they, as always, are the key to Amazon's extraordinary growth.

TAKEAWAYS

- Jeff Bezos created a firm obsessively focused on customers, based on a strategic flywheel that has resulted in explosive growth.
- He starts with providing the things that customers always want—more choice, lower prices, and faster delivery.
- Amazon also invests heavily in innovation, creating products and services that customers don't know they need but soon come to value.
- Bezos, perhaps as much as any leader of a large corporation, is focused on his firm's culture—intent on sustaining the benefits of what he calls "Day 1."

4 BUILDING GREAT PRODUCTS: ELON MUSK & TESLA

An obsessive nature with respect to the
quality of the product is very important
and so being an obsessive compulsive is
a good thing in this context.[1]

—Elon Musk

The public is fascinated by Elon Musk's accomplishments as well as
his provocative personality—with twenty-two million people following
him on Twitter. How many leaders have done things that NASA, with
its government funding and decades of experience, could not do? At
the same time, how many leaders conduct an interview where they
appear to be drinking whiskey and smoking marijuana? In a world
where most CEOs work hard to avoid controversy, Musk courts it. But
we pay attention to Musk because he has brought to life some of the
most innovative and highly regarded products ever imagined. Like the
namesake of his car company, Musk sees himself as the creator of useful
things that will result in a better future for humanity. Over his career
he has built billion-dollar companies in capital intensive industries,
going up against well-established, well-resourced firms:

- *Tesla* has won numerous automotive awards for the quality
  of its vehicles. Motor Trend named Tesla's Model S its car of

the year for 2013, saying it is "proof positive that America can still make (great) things."[2] Another reviewer wrote that a later version of the car "performed better in our tests than any other car ever has, breaking the Consumer Reports Ratings system."[3]

- *SpaceX* is the first private company to send a liquid fuel rocket around the earth and the first to send a spacecraft to dock with the International Space Station. In another first, the firm launched a reusable rocket that returned to Earth and landed on a drone ship in the Atlantic, offering more affordable space exploration and commerce. The company's long-term goal is to produce a spacecraft capable of traveling to Mars.
- *Solar City* is pioneering the use of solar energy for public consumption. It installs solar panels on residential and commercial buildings. It also builds large solar complexes, having completed a massive facility in Australia capable of powering thirty-thousand homes in the case of a blackout.
- *PayPal* is the pioneering online payment system that Musk and his partners sold to eBay for $1.5 billion in 2002. Today PayPal is the leader in third-party online payments with almost 300 million active users.[4]
- *Boring* is a start-up transportation company in the early stages of developing underground systems capable of moving people and products in urban areas at exceptional speeds (currently at 288 mph but with a potential top speed of 760 mph).[5] The company is now testing prototypes in Los Angeles and Las Vegas.

Creating revolutionary products was important to Musk early in his career, as evident in his leadership of two ventures. Looking back, he said, "We were really very focused on building the best product that we possibly could. Both Zip2 and PayPal were very product-focused companies. We were incredibly obsessive about how do we evoke something that is really going to be the best possible customer experience. And that was a far more effective selling tool than having a giant sales force or thinking of marketing gimmicks or twelve-step processes or whatever."[6] Musk believes that companies that create shoddy products will struggle and likely fail—and points to the US car manufacturers as a case in point. Instead, he designs his cars to be innovative and exciting—a significant accomplishment in a country whose automotive companies have struggled to remain solvent in the face of foreign competition. A venture capitalist who invests in technology firms holds views similar to Musk and suggests that an all-consuming product focus is the key to business success:

> The great companies that I've been an investor in share a common trait—the founder/CEO is obsessed with the product. Not interested, not aware of, not familiar with, but *obsessed*. Every discussion trends back toward the product. All of the conversations about customers are really about how the customer uses the product and the value the product brings the customer. The majority of the early teams are focused entirely on the product, including the non-engineering people. Product, product, product.[7]

Contrast this to what occurs in many companies as they grow. Steve Jobs noted that successful companies often create layer after layer of middle managers, which isolate the senior leaders from those performing the detailed work of product development, engineering, and manufacturing. As a result, "They no longer have an inherent feel or a passion about the products. The creative people, who are the ones who care passionately, have to persuade five layers of management to do what they know is the right thing to do."[8] The result is a company that can live for a while off past achievements but lacks the focus and drive needed to develop future generations of desirable products. Jobs thought of profit as that which flowed from great products—it was never the goal in itself. He told his biographer, "My passion has been to build an enduring company where people were motivated to make great products . . . the products, not the profits, were the motivation."[9]

Musk estimates that he spends 80 percent of his time on design and engineering challenges. He is also a savvy marketer who knows how to attract attention to his products to generate customer demand. In his quest to develop support for a rocket that can travel to Mars, Musk placed a Tesla on a SpaceX Falcon rocket. He seated a mannequin in the driver's seat of the car and, once launched, made public a photo of "Spaceman" sitting in the Tesla inside the rocket as it raced past Earth. On the dashboard of the car were the words "Don't Panic." The rocket will likely be in orbit for hundreds of millions of years. Another example of Musk's marketing mind-set is the design of his products. The most powerful version of the Tesla S can accelerate from 0 to 60 mph in 2.27 seconds—which is exceptionally fast for any car but particularly an electric car. To achieve this level of acceleration, the driver activates an option on the car's control screen that reads "ludicrous acceleration."[10]

Despite its innovative automobiles, the fate of Tesla is still uncertain. Musk, until recently, has repeatedly failed to deliver on Tesla's production and profitability promises, which eroded support for him, his company, and its stock price. The *Wall Street Journal* noted that, over five years, Musk missed ten of his publicly espoused goals by almost one year on average.[11] His pattern of overpromising and other factors, including increased competition from the likes of VW, have made Tesla one of the most shorted stocks on the US exchange—meaning that many smart people are betting that his company will fail. Even Musk has stated that the probability of him being successful in building a mainstream car company is only 10 percent.

In 2019, Tesla gained momentum in meeting its production targets and opening a new plant in China in record time. It became the most valuable car company in the history of the US. Yet, there are widely divergent views on the future of the company. But even his critics must admit that Musk doesn't back away from audacious challenges—and the risks of doing so. He said he took the profit from the sale of PayPal and put it into three new ventures—$100 million in SpaceX, $70 million in Tesla, and $10 million in Solar City. Musk believes it is wrong to use other people's money on risky ventures if he is unwilling to invest his own money. Looking back on the decision to do so, he noted, "Most people, when they make a lot of money, don't want to risk it. For me it was never about money but solving problems for the future of humanity."[12]

BUILD SOMETHING THAT MATTERS

Musk's obsession with products starts with building things that will benefit society: "I'm interested in things that change the world or that affect the future and wondrous, new technology where you see it, and you're like, 'Wow, how did that even happen? How is that possible?'"[13] If the use of electric cars becomes widespread because of Tesla's impact, it will reduce the damage to the environment from internal combustion engines. Solar panels will reduce the harmful impact of conventional power plants, particularly those burning coal. According to Musk, SpaceX will provide the means for us to become a multiplanetary species. Products that matter, however, are not always revolutionary. Some just make life easier and more rewarding for as many people as possible. For instance, PayPal was useful in facilitating online purchases, a relatively minor contribution compared to building rockets with the intent of allowing people to colonize Mars. In encouraging other entrepreneurs, Musk says the first goal in a product-centric company must be to build something that contributes to the well-being of others—in small or significant ways.

Many companies, especially in the tech industry, claim their goal is to make the world a better place. Facebook's mission is "to give people the power to share and make the world more open and connected." However, some argue, particularly given how Facebook has managed data privacy concerns, that the company is more focused on getting as many people as possible to use and stay on its site, learn as much as possible about them, and then use that information to generate ad revenue. User information is Facebook's most valuable asset—allowing it to provide targeted advertising to those who will pay dearly to reach specific customer sets.[14] While doing good and making money are not mutually exclusive, Facebook's actions suggest that growth and profit are central to how it operates.

It is hard to make the same criticism of Tesla or SpaceX. Musk's companies are truly mission-driven, with big dreams and potentially huge consequences if they succeed. Electric vehicles, for example, were on the market for years before Musk. Few people wanted to own one because of their limited range, poor driving experience, and unattractive design. If you drove an electric car pre-Tesla, you did so because you were a committed environmentalist (and, as a result, willing to drive an inferior vehicle). Tesla then changed everything in offering an electric car that was fast and attractive, becoming a status symbol for reasons beyond being electric, and revitalizing the EV segment of the car industry.[15] Musk claims he wants other manufacturers to follow his lead in producing electric cars because, "We're running the most dangerous experiment in history right now, which is to see how much carbon dioxide the atmosphere . . . can handle before there is an environmental catastrophe."[16] Other car manufacturers, such as VW, Mercedes, and Ford, are now ramping up their efforts to produce and market electric vehicles after years of ignoring the category. GM will introduce twenty electric cars in the next four years. Musk disrupted the automotive industry and may become the victim of his success as larger competitors erode his first-mover advantage.

STRIVE FOR SUPERIOR UTILITY, RELIABILITY & BEAUTY

Musk is the CEO and lead designer/product architect at SpaceX and Tesla. He believes that those with engineering and design expertise should lead companies—versus the more common CEO career path through finance, marketing, or sales.[17] Musk believes CEOs, at least in product focused firms, should work primarily on design and engineering challenges. He noted that what is obvious to him in solving tough problems is not obvious to most people. The result, in the ideal, is a product that is significantly better than what currently exists. He writes,

> If you're entering anything where there's an existing marketplace against large, entrenched competitors, then your product or service needs to be much better than theirs. . . . You're always going to buy the trusted brand unless there's a big difference. . . . It can't just be slightly better, it's gotta be a lot better.[18]

Musk, like Jobs, puts products first. As a result, he redirects money spent on other areas, such as marketing, to the critical areas of product design and manufacturing. He describes the common mistakes that leaders and companies make in paying attention to the noise over the signal—which results in wasted efforts and a lack of focus on what truly matters:

> A lot of companies get confused. They spend money on things that don't actually make the product better. So, for example, at Tesla we've never spent any money on advertising. We put all the money into R&D and manufacturing and design to try to make the car as good as possible. And I think that's the way to go, so for any given company, just keep thinking about, "Are these efforts that people are expending, are they resulting in a better product or service?," and if they're not, stop those efforts.[19]

Making a better product involves three goals—the product is compelling in providing something better than what currently exists, it performs reliably over time, and it is beautiful (what Musk sometimes describes as "sexy"). Design, in this respect, is much more than how something looks—much more than its veneer. It is how it works in total.[20] Musk creates vehicles that strive to maximize all three goals and, as a result, they have very high customer satisfaction ratings. He writes, "We're in pursuit of the platonic ideal of the perfect car. Who knows what that looks like actually, but you want to try to make every element of the car as flawless as possible. There will always be some degree of imperfection, but we try to minimize that and create a car that is just delightful in every way."[21]

For instance, Tesla cars are powered by a battery that, when introduced, was far superior to anything then on the market. It used the lithium-ion technology found in smaller electronic devices such as phones and computers. These batteries are lighter and more powerful, and advances in manufacturing continue to make them less expensive. The right configuration of lithium-ion batteries allowed the first Model S to travel upwards of 265 miles on a single charge, more than twice what was then available in other electric cars and closer to the per-tank distance found in many gasoline-powered vehicles. This reduced the "range anxiety" that limited the popularity of electric cars. Perhaps equally important, the new technology resulted in an incredibly fast car.

Musk didn't stop with creating a better battery. Aesthetics matter to Musk and he tells his people, "If you're going to make a product, make it beautiful. Even if it doesn't affect sales, I want it to be beautiful."[22] His attention to aesthetics is evident in Tesla's door handles. He wanted a distinctive handle—one that would extend for the driver when he or she approached the vehicle and then recess into the door panel when driven. It sounds simple enough. However, the reason we don't see this type of door handle on most cars is that it is incredibly complicated to design and manufacture. The handle needs to work reliably or the driver can't get into the car. This requires that it perform consistently over thousands of uses under a variety of conditions (heat, cold, ice, rain). The handle also needs to be safe—stopping if a passenger's finger becomes inadvertently caught as it closes. Despite pushback from some of his engineers, Musk achieved what he wanted with the handle, which has become a signature feature of his cars.

In this respect, Musk is similar to Steve Jobs in emphasizing the critical role of product design in a company's success. Both men indicated that great companies are the result of great products. In a telling comment, Jobs said that he had no issue with Microsoft's hard-earned success. The major objection he had was that the company produced what Jobs saw as third-rate products that lacked both originality and aesthetically desirable features. He suggested that the problem with Microsoft under the leadership of Gates and Ballmer was that its people weren't in love with what they created.

THINK BOLDLY, THEN OBSESS ON THE DETAILS

Musk obsessively focuses on breakthrough technical ideas. He describes his mind as "a never-ending explosion" of ideas that he can't turn off. "There are times, late at night, when I pace. . . . If I'm trying to solve a problem, and I think I've got some elements of it kind of close to being figured out, I'll pace for hours trying to think it through."[23] As noted above, the company's founders and Musk had the insight that batteries made with lithium, what Tesla calls the Li-ion energy system, would be far superior to anything then on the market. This battery allows cars to accelerate much faster and have a longer life span than more traditional nickel or lead acid-based batteries. But it is expensive and would only be an option for use in a car by reducing cost through design and manufacturing innovations. Once Musk decided on the benefit of the Li-ion battery, he focused on the hard work of mass-producing it in a cost-effective manner.

This same breakthrough mind-set is conspicuous at SpaceX. Musk decided that reusable rockets would reduce the cost of space travel and transport (and make achievements such as travel to Mars economically feasible). Many in the space industry believed it was impossible to design such a rocket. Not even NASA, with decades of experience and vast government support, had produced a reusable rocket but that did not deter Musk. A colleague said that Musk, with no prior experience in rocket design or manufacturing, consumed textbooks and technical manuals on the subject, and sought out industry luminaries to tutor him. He also hired some of the best in the industry and extracted what they knew. One employee noted, "I thought at first that he was challenging me to see if I knew my stuff. Then I realized he was trying to learn things. He would quiz you until he learned ninety percent of what you know."[24] Musk's learning, however, was not simply absorbing what others had done or said. He challenged assumptions—such as the feasibility of a reusable rocket. One of his colleagues said that Musk would regularly challenge highly regarded experts in the field, with some being insulted by the assertions of someone new to their industry.[25] They saw him as a novice—naïve about what was possible in an industry in which he had no experience.

Musk, like Bezos and Jobs, believes that developing break-through ideas is only the start of creating something revolutionary. It also requires a leader to dive into the design and manufacturing details because great products are built on hundreds—if not thousands—of details. Management experts typically argue against Musk's approach—suggesting that senior leaders should avoid getting into the operational minutiae because it takes time away from more strategic work that only they can do. Executives getting into the details can also demoralize those doing the work since they believe that they, not those in more senior roles, should be managing the areas assigned to them.

In contrast, Musk believes that leaders who don't get involved are being negligent and their products suffer as a result. He proudly describes himself as a "nano-manager"—one who knows that details matter. This is his way of saying that he goes beyond what some call micromanagement and instead practices "a hands-on obsession with the tiniest operational and car-design details at Tesla."[26] His deep product knowledge informs not only his design decisions but also the execution of his vision—including manufacturing, logistics, and marketing. Musk argues that business is akin to fighting a battle, and leaders need to be on the front lines with their troops versus sitting in an office with only a limited understanding of the product being built and sold.

SEEK FEEDBACK, PARTICULARLY NEGATIVE FEEDBACK

Musk believes that firms will stagnate if they assume that their product is good enough to sustain or grow market share. Instead, companies need to continually improve their products or another firm will introduce a better product—and take their customers.[27] One example of his approach is evident in how Musk responded to the initial manufacturing runs of Tesla. He examined the vehicles as they came off the assembly line, looking for the smallest variance from what he wanted. He noticed details that most CEOs would miss or delegate to others—the slightest misalignment of a tail lamp or piece of trim, a body panel that increased slightly from top to bottom, a paint finish with slight inconsistencies. Musk told one interviewer that finding such relatively minor flaws in the Tesla was like someone putting daggers in his eyes.[28]

One of the ways that Musk improves his products is to ask users for negative feedback. His behavior when doing so is somewhat surprising because he can be defensive when believing that someone has slighted him, his firm, or its products. He has stated that seeking negative feedback on the smallest aspects of his products is essential in making the product as good as it can be—noting that "It's easy to 'get high on your own supply,' as Scarface said. You've gotta not be afraid to innovate, but also don't delude yourself into thinking something's working when it's not, or you're going to get fixated on a bad solution."[29] He believes the best feedback is often from friends because they care about him. But sometimes they will not be honest because they don't want to offend him. So Musk goes out of his way to obtain their input, suggesting that savvy leaders seek negative feedback even when others don't want to provide it. He is most interested in talking with customers about what is missing or wrong with his cars. Customers and friends describing what they like doesn't help make the car better. He knows a car's strengths but may be less aware of what they see as its weaknesses.

WORK HARD, REALLY HARD

Musk believes that success in creating revolutionary products demands an unrelenting work ethic. He tells those who want to emulate his success that they should work until late in the night and then dream about their products while sleeping. Do this for seven days a week with no vacations and no breaks.[30] In a commencement speech he gave to graduating students of USC, he gave the following advice on building a successful company:

> I think the first is . . . you need to work super hard. So what does *super hard* mean? Well, when my brother and I were starting our first company, instead of getting an apartment, we just rented a small office and we slept on the couch and we showered in the YMCA. We were so hard up that we

had just one computer. So the website was up during the day, and I was coding at night. 7 days a week, all the time. . . . So, work hard, like, every waking hour.[31]

Musk's exceptional work ethic is ingrained in each of his companies. Commenting on the mission of Tesla and SpaceX, he notes, "You're not going to create revolutionary cars or rockets on 40 hours a week. It just won't work. Colonizing Mars isn't going to happen on 40 hours a week."[32] A typical week for him begins at Space X in Los Angeles, followed by several days at Tesla in Northern California and then back to SpaceX on Friday. Some weeks also include a trip to Nevada to spend time at Solar City. In a recent interview he noted that he spent three to four days in a row at Tesla without leaving the facility. He needed to be present with his team to solve the manufacturing problems with the Model 3. When not in the office or on the plant floor, Musk is almost always accessible to his people. He tells them that they should not hesitate to reach out to him, when necessary, saying, "I'm available 24/7 to help solve issues. Call me at 3:00 a.m. on a Sunday morning. I don't care."[33]

Musk's obsession with his work is apparent in a comment he made to a friend while he was still in college: "If there was a way that I could not eat, so I could work more, I would not eat. I wish there was a way to get nutrients without sitting down for a meal."[34] His friend remembered being surprised by the comment, thinking it unusual in its intensity. Others who have worked with Musk make similar observations, suggesting that one of his defining traits is his complete commitment to his work. A biographer wrote, "The biggest thing people miss is his level of resolve and commitment. I've interviewed all these people in Silicon Valley, and I just never met anyone like him. For most people, even if they're a really passionate CEO, it's still a job. But for Elon, it's somewhere between a life-or-death struggle and a war."[35]

Musk is not alone in his work ethic. Steve Jobs said that the Apple Mac team worked fourteen to eighteen hours a day, seven days a week—and did so for two-plus years. He said the team members were young, loved their work, and could put in the hours needed to create a revolutionary product. Bill Gates said the same was true throughout his twenties, as he and Paul Allen built Microsoft.[36] The same for Travis Kalanick at Uber and Jack Ma at Alibaba. Work-life balance is absent in many of the greatest success stories of the past few decades.

BUILD YOUR SPECIAL FORCES

Musk has noted that Tesla, as well as his other firms, focus on hiring highly talented people in key areas such as product engineering and manufacturing. He has stated that some companies fail, particularly in technology-intensive areas, because they don't have a critical mass of talented people:

> The ability to attract and motivate great people is critical to the success of a company because a company is a group of people that are assembled to create a product or service. That's the purpose of a company. People sometimes forget this elementary truth. If you're able to get great people to join the company and work together toward a common goal and have a relentless sense of perfection about that goal, then you will end up with a great product.[37]

In contrast, Musk believes that most large firms develop bureaucratic processes that become more important than having the smart and creative people needed to deliver results.[38] Musk wants a cadre of talented colleagues who are deeply committed to achieving a shared goal. Like

Bezos, he values the mentality found in successful entrepreneurial firms at their inception:

> I want to accentuate the philosophy that I have with companies in the startup phase, which is a sort of special forces approach. The minimum passing grade is excellent. That's the way I believe startup companies need to be if they're ultimately going to be large and successful companies. We'd adhered to that to some degree, but we'd strayed from that path in a few places. That doesn't mean the people that we let go on that basis would be considered bad—it's just the difference between Special Forces and regular Army. If you're going to get through a really tough environment and ultimately grow the company to something significant, you have to have a very high level of dedication and talent throughout the organization.[39]

Musk will personally interview employees for technical positions, including those who will assume roles lower in the organization's hierarchy. He reportedly interviewed the pool of candidates for the first two hundred engineers hired at SpaceX. In his interviews, he wants to hear about the problems they faced and how they solved them. But he doesn't want general statements about outcomes—he wants rich details about what was done, believing that those who truly solved the problem never forget what was involved in doing so.[40] Musk also assesses potential hires on their willingness to put in the effort that he believes is necessary to achieve something exceptional. One common interview question at Tesla is, "We work long hours and weekends at Tesla. You're probably used to a more 9 to 5 type job. How do you feel about the expectation of working long hours?"[41] Musk says, "If you are working at Tesla, you're choosing to step up your game. And that has pluses and minuses. It's cool to be

Special Forces, but it also means you're working your ass off. It's not for everyone."[42]

PRODUCT-CENTRIC DOWNSIDES

Musk's obsession with creating amazing products has significant downsides, some with the potential to undermine his remarkable achievements.

Work Over Life: The intensity of being completely consumed with one's work fits Musk's personality. One of his colleagues described Musk as a machine—working around the clock, not taking vacations for years, and dividing his time each week among the three companies he leads. To those who suggest that he take breaks and decompress, he says, "The idea of lying on a beach as my main thing just sounds like the worst—it sounds horrible to me. I would go bonkers. I would have to be on serious drugs. I'd be super-duper bored. I like high intensity."[43] By Musk's admission, he pushes himself to the point of physically and mentally breaking down. Tesla has faced life-threatening periods several times during its history, as has SpaceX. In a 2018 interview with the *New York Times*, Musk became emotional when describing the stress he is under to make Tesla a success.[44] Experiencing what he calls the worst year of his career, he struggled as the company worked to meet aggressive production targets for the Tesla Model 3. The company needs to produce and sell enough cars to meet the financial obligations of operating while also paying down its significant debt. Musk notes,

> A lot of times people think creating companies is going to
> be fun. I would say it's not. It's really not that fun. There
> are periods of fun, and there are periods where it's just

awful. Particularly if you're the CEO of the company, you actually have a distillation of all the worst problems in the company. There's no point in spending your time on things that are going right, so you only spend your time on things that are going wrong . . . I think you have to feel quite compelled to do it and have a fairly high pain threshold.[45]

Musk admits that his extreme workload has played a role in his making ill-advised statements that hurt him and his firm. His controversial behavior resulted in some stating that he had become a liability—that he didn't have the temperament to lead effectively.[46] An investment firm that has previously backed Musk said that it would not continue to invest in Tesla, at least in the near-term, because of what they describe as Musk's reckless actions.[47] An analyst downgraded the stock, he wrote, "The issue though is the erratic behavior of CEO Elon Musk. . . . We are worried that his behavior is tainting the Tesla brand, which in terms of value is most important."[48] Another Wall Street pundit, commenting on Musk's reported use of marijuana during an interview, suggested that "this is the behavior of a man who should not be running a public company."[49]

Creativity Over Process: Product-centric leaders can be opposed to process. They prefer creative people who design innovative products and, in so doing, solve difficult challenges. Musk has stated that he doesn't trust process, which he views as a bureaucratic response to complex problems that are best solved by smart and resourceful people. He writes,

I don't believe in process. In fact, when I interview a potential employee and he or she says that "it's all about the process," I see that as a bad sign. The problem is that at a lot of big companies, process becomes a substitute for thinking. You're encouraged to behave like a little gear in a complex machine. Frankly, it allows you to keep people who aren't that smart, who aren't that creative.[50]

Musk has a degree in physics and views himself as an engineer above all else. The question is if he can bring his talents to bear not only on product design but manufacturing. He has proven that he can design extraordinary things, but some doubt that he can build them on a mass level. Tesla has made significant progress in meeting its production goals but will need to demonstrate that it can be sustained.

Contrast Musk's approach to what Steve Jobs did at Apple. He delegated Apple's production work to Tim Cook, who made sure the company produced the volume and quality of products that Apple needed. Jobs remained focus on design and marketing, while Cook effectively managed the operational side of the business, including contracting with vendors with the capabilities to meet Apple's high standards. To date, Musk does not have someone at Tesla who can do what Tim Cook did for Jobs.[51] Musk appears to have turned the corner in resolving many of the manufacturing issues that limited production of the Model 3. Those who underestimated Musk in the past have been proven wrong. But the challenges will increase as his firm becomes larger and faces new competition. Experts in manufacturing agree that superior performance requires robust organizational processes, along with an experienced and disciplined process leader.

Products Over Colleagues: Successful entrepreneurs build teams and organizations capable of turning their ideas into reality. The challenge is that obsessive leaders, particularly those who are product-centric, may care more about their creations than anything else—including their coworkers. They are often tough on those who work for them—setting audacious goals and treating colleagues harshly when things don't go as planned. Like other well-known entrepreneurs such as Jobs and Bezos, Musk has little patience for those who lack the talent or commitment needed to deliver at the highest level.

According to Musk, companies exist solely to get things done in the building of great products. This can be inspirational for those who share his passion, but his total commitment can also result in a highly stressful work environment. There are clear benefits to setting and enforcing high standards—even standards that others view as unrealistic. The downside of Musk's management philosophy is a work culture under constant pressure, with employees working long hours in pursuit of ambitious targets. For example, Tesla set an eighteen-month goal to produce five hundred thousand Model 3 cars a year, which is a tenfold increase over its prior production rate. The result was a period of what Musk called "production hell." One colleague summarized Elon's relentless drive to achieve his goals: "Elon does not know about you, and he has not thought through whether or not something is going to hurt your feelings. He just knows what the fuck he wants to be done. People who did not normalize to his communication style did not do well."[52] Take Musk's approach to those who didn't measure up at one of his first companies. Looking back on the experience, he said,

> Yeah, we had some very good software engineers at Zip2, but I mean, I could code way better than them. And I'd just go in and fix their fucking code . . . I would be frustrated waiting for their stuff, so I'm going to go and fix your code and now it runs five times faster, you idiot. There was one guy who wrote a quantum mechanics equation, a quantum probability on the board, and he

got it wrong. I'm like, "How can you write that?" Then I corrected it for him. He hated me after that. Eventually, I realized, Okay, I might have fixed that thing but now I've made the person unproductive. It just wasn't a good way to go about things.[53]

Musk is known to harshly criticize his colleagues when they fail to meet his expectations. An employee who worked with him in one of his first ventures observed, "You would see people come out of the meetings with this disgusted look on their face. You don't get to where Elon is now by always being a nice guy, and he was just so driven and sure of himself."[54] Another former colleague noted that the experience of working at Tesla was incredible but that he would never work there again due to the unrelenting demands that Musk placed on himself and his coworkers.[55] Ashlee Vance, who wrote a detailed and mostly laudatory biography of Elon Musk, concluded that "his brand of empathy is unique. He seems to feel for the human species as a whole, without always wanting to consider the wants and needs of individuals."[56]

One sign that Musk is pushing hard, perhaps too hard, is the high level of turnover in key Tesla executive positions. By one account, eighty-eight executives left Tesla over a one-year period beginning in January 2018, some on their own accord and others fired by Musk.[57] Among those departing include the firm's chief financial officer, engineering head, chief accounting officer, director of engineering, vice president of worldwide service, vice president of autopilot, director of performance engineering, and chief people officer. The turnover has alarmed some investors, who suggest that Musk's management style does not scale—that his intense and hands-on approach results in talented people leaving the company. A Musk biographer claimed that one employee complained that the work hours were excessive and keeping him from seeing his family. Reportedly, Musk said that the colleague would see a great deal of his family if the company went bankrupt.[58] Musk denied making this statement despite his belief in the need for his people to be wholly committed to the work and the success of the company.

THE THOMAS EDISON OF OUR AGE?

Obsession has the potential, when combined with a creative intellect, to take a leader and his or her organization to amazing heights. Tesla is now emerging from a period of turmoil, and Musk has silenced some of his most vocal critics. But we are not sure if history will view Musk as this generation's Thomas Edison or its Nikola Tesla. Musk admires both but reveres Thomas Edison, as noted when asked his views of their achievements:

> The car company is called Tesla . . . because we use an AC induction motor, which is an architecture that Tesla developed. And the guy probably deserves a little more play than he gets in current society. But on balance, I'm a bigger fan of Edison than Tesla because Edison brought his stuff to market and made those inventions accessible to the world, whereas Tesla didn't really do that.[59]

We still don't know how much play Elon Musk will receive in a future that he is determined to improve. In 2019, the company performed at high level—and is now worth more than GM and Ford combined. The question is can he, and the team around him, manage the downsides of his obsessive personality—one that has brought him and his companies so far?

TAKEAWAYS

- Elon Musk believes great companies are built on great products. Everything in a firm should focus on making delightful products that make a difference to society.
- He is a technological visionary who believes in "leading from the front"—being intimately involved in the design and operational details of the firms he leads and the products they are creating.
- His goal is to build an organization staffed at all levels by highly talented and motivated people, particularly in the design and engineering functions.
- Musk pushes himself and his team to the absolute limit—and in so doing risks undermining what he has achieved.

5

JUICING GROWTH:

TRAVIS KALANICK & UBER

Travis's biggest strength is that he will
run through a wall to accomplish his goals.
Travis's biggest weakness is that he will
run through a wall to accomplish his goals.[1]

—Mark Cuban

Travis Kalanick spent his childhood in a nondescript suburb of Los
Angeles. His father, a civil engineer, recognized the growing importance of information technology and bought his children the best
computers.[2] His mother, an advertising sales executive, was equally
influential in encouraging Travis to get involved in various entrepreneurial activities. He peddled steak knives door-to-door at age ten, sold
tickets to charity events as a teen, and founded a college preparatory
business in his final year of high school. Travis, a math nerd who was
proud of his ability to outhustle others, showed early signs of what he
would become—a serial tech entrepreneur.

Kalanick enrolled at UCLA to study computer engineering but was
more excited about starting a company than finishing his degree. He
quit school in his senior year to join a small start-up founded by several of his classmates. The company, Scour, was an early peer-to-peer
file-sharing service. Similar to the more infamous Napster, it allowed
people to exchange popular media via the internet. It fit the stereotype

of a chaotic, small start-up company, run by a group of bright, ambitious, and inexperienced entrepreneurs. One of the firm's employees said, "It was very, very scrappy and none of us knew what we were doing."[3] Offering popular movies and music for free was an easy sell and Kalanick was an excellent salesman. The company soon had millions of users. The problem was that media companies, who produced the movies and music that Kalanick's customers were downloading, believed Scour was stealing their intellectual property. They went to court to shut down his company, suing for $250 billion in damages. Facing a massive fine, which Kalanick wryly noted exceeded the gross domestic product of Sweden, Scour wisely filed for bankruptcy.

It wasn't long before Kalanick started another firm. Red Swoosh sold enterprise software to transfer files by taking advantage of the unused computing power of the desktop machines owned by end-users. Kalanick's target customer was the group of companies that had forced Scour out of business—media firms that wanted to send large files such as movies faster and cheaper via the internet. Kalanick had no problem seeking the business of those who had killed his company. He said, "The idea was to take those 33 litigants that sued me and turn them into customers. So, now those dudes who are suing me are paying me."[4]

For the next seven years, Kalanick dealt with a host of technical, managerial, and financial challenges. Red Swoosh owed $110,000 to the IRS for income taxes that were not withheld from employee paychecks. Kalanick blamed his partner for failing to pay the taxes, while his partner claimed that Kalanick was in on the decision not to do so (and instead to use the money to run the business). Kalanick found new investors to pay the IRS, avoiding potential jail time. Red Swoosh survived only because of Kalanick's resilience in persisting through one setback after another. His cofounder quit and a deal to sell the company fell through. When asked why he stayed with it, including moving back into his parents' home and working for three years without a salary, Kalanick said that he couldn't control who he fell in love with—even if he was in love with an abusive partner.[5] His resilience paid off when Red Swoosh was sold to Akamai for $19 million, with Kalanick personally gaining an estimated $3 million from the deal.[6]

Kalanick spent the next year traveling the world, enjoying a hard-earned vacation and determining his next move. He settled in San Francisco and invested in several start-up ventures, searching for ideas that met his "awesomeness" criteria (a business plan that excited him when talking about it to others). One intriguing idea was the brainchild of Garret Camp, a Canadian-born entrepreneur who had recently sold his firm StumbleUpon to eBay. Camp and Kalanick socialized in the same circles,[7] gathering with like-minded entrepreneurs to exchange ideas for new businesses.

Camp's start-up company was the result of his experiences living in San Francisco. He owned a car but didn't like to drive in the city. Instead, he took taxis but service in the city was unreliable, as the number of taxis in San Francisco had lagged far behind the demand. Camp grew frustrated with being unable to quickly find a cab. He started calling for a car via taxi dispatch but was impatient when it didn't arrive promptly. His solution was to call several services and take the first car that arrived.[8] Eventually the taxi companies grew tired of Camp's no-shows and refused to provide him with service.

Camp thought there must be a better way to match cars with riders and reduce waiting times. The newly introduced iPhone had a motion sensor that, when used with the phone's GPS, could track a driver as he or she moved through a city. Seeing the business potential, Camp designed an app to coordinate the location of cars and riders, which shortened pick-up times. The app would also allow for accurate estimates of the total trip cost before a ride took place. He called his new company Uber-Cab, with the confidence that comes from offering a service that you know is superior to anything provided by your competitors.

Camp believed Kalanick could take his fledgling company and maximize its growth potential. He tells the story of when they were in Paris for a conference and decided to walk up the Eiffel Tower. To Camp's surprise, Kalanick hopped over barriers to get a better view of the city. "I liked that quality of going for it," recalls Camp. "I knew such a big idea would take a lot of guts, and he impressed me as someone who had that."[9] A journalist, commenting on Kalanick's personality and the combative nature of his firm, noted that "Uber really was born as a vicious pit bull that believed it would spend its life in the ring."[10]

Camp and Kalanick had different ideas on what UberCab should become. They both realized that Camp's software was groundbreaking. However, Camp was intent on building a fleet of limos to provide a high-end luxury service for those who wanted something better than either yellow cabs or conventional black cars. His company was more expensive than a cab but provided a faster and more reliable service. Kalanick argued that a low-cost, high-quality service was better because it could grow into a huge company. The motto of the service would be "Everyone's Private Driver." Lower fares, argued Kalanick, would result in more customers and they would create demand that would result in more cars on the road, which in turn would result in faster pickup times and more money for drivers. The lower-cost approach would result in better service than the traditional, high-end luxury offering. Consultants refer to this as a "virtuous cycle" where success in one area feeds success in another, resulting in an ever-expanding positive loop. Kalanick believed that his business model would fundamentally change how people moved from one point to another in cities around the world. He saw that the upside potential was far beyond that of a technology-aided limo service for the wealthy in cities such as San Francisco.

Kalanick's other big idea was to build the business with independent drivers using their cars (versus building a fleet of company cars with full-time employees). The idea was similar in some respects to Red Swoosh, which leveraged a desktop's unused computing power. Kalanick wanted to tap the unused potential of others' cars. Perhaps more importantly, using independent drivers would allow Kalanick and Camp to claim that Uber was not a taxi company but a technology firm providing software that supported self-employed drivers. In the minds of its founders, contracting rather than employing drivers would allow Uber to grow without facing the myriad of regulations and restrictions that stifled taxi competition in most cities and municipalities. Camp agreed with Kalanick's plan and gave him equity that eventually made him the firm's largest individual shareholder.[11] Uber, with Kalanick as its CEO, was on its way to becoming one of the most valuable companies in the emerging on-demand, one-click economy.

Riders immediately embraced Uber and the company quickly expanded in each new city it entered. Customers could push a button on their phone and get a car in a matter of minutes. No more chasing down a yellow cab on a city street or calling a black car in advance. No need to guess how much your trip would cost. No need for cash or a credit card since the billing was automated. The benefits of what Kalanick called a "low-cost luxury" were undeniable and the firm expanded at a rapid rate. Uber's primary competitor, Lyft, was also offering rides but by owners in everyday cars—not black cars, as was the case in the early years of Uber.

Lyft's founders observed during a trip to Africa that it was common for people to give each other lifts in their cars—sharing rides in a manner that would benefit both drivers and riders.[12] Kalanick initially resisted Lyft's approach, telling regulators that allowing drivers to use any car in a ride-sharing service was unsafe (in comparison to using newer black cars). As Lyft's service gained popularity, Kalanick shifted his position and adopted ridesharing for Uber. As a result, Uber became one of the fastest growing start-ups in history, at one point valued at $75 billion just ten years after its founding.[13] The company now employs twenty-two thousand people, has a global network of 3.9 million drivers, and provides rides to 14 million people a day.[14] It sees itself as the future of transportation.

THE INNOVATOR'S PLAYGROUND

Kalanick views himself as a creative pragmatist focused on solving real-world problems. He compares himself to a mathematician, one who prefers difficult problems. "What drives me is a hard problem that hasn't been solved, that has a really interesting and impactful solution."[15] He describes the "innovator's playground" as the area in which conventional wisdom is wrong, providing an enormous opportunity for those who are creative and tenacious.[16] This requires seeing opportunities when others see impossibilities. It also requires the ability to execute one's ideas in the face of adversity. The challenge, and anxiety, that comes with achieving what others believe is impossible is what Kalanick called the drug of choice for people like himself.[17]

Ridesharing was designed to provide a faster, cheaper, and safer way from point A to point B. But two significant challenges faced Kalanick and his team. The first was technical: determining how to get cars to people as efficiently as possible, despite the complexities of city traffic and widely varying consumer demand. The technical challenge required sophisticated logistical planning, software that placed cars where people would need them, and the right number of drivers. The goal was to match supply with demand so that people would be in a car within five minutes of pushing the Uber icon on their phone.

The second problem, even more challenging, was political. Few believed that it was possible to compete with taxi and limo services that operated as a monopoly in almost every US city and town—an arrangement that Kalanick labeled the "taxi cartel."[18] The political challenge required that Uber go up against a broad range of influential stakeholders that supported one of the most regulated industries in the world. He would face fierce and well-funded resistance from taxi authorities, taxi/limo drivers, and the local and state politicians who support them. Kalanick's strategy was to offer a service so exceptional that the public would put pressure on local governments to allow access to it. He developed an Uber launch playbook that was refined over time and used in each city it entered. For example, the mayor of New York wanted to restrict Uber's operations in his city. However, the mayor was forced to back down after Uber launched a massive public relations campaign that resulted in thousands of residents requesting that he not restrict Uber's service in the city. To create change, Kalanick was willing to alienate powerful special-interest groups along the way. He also hired a legion of lobbyists and public relations firms to advance his cause. In his mind, a larger good was being served—and a wrong was being righted.

Uber's rapid growth meant that Kalanick was soon in charge of a highly visible firm. Like many well-known technology founders, such as Mark Zuckerberg and Jeff Bezos, Kalanick was learning how to lead while leading. Managing a large and complex enterprise was far beyond what he experienced at Scour and Red Swoosh. He looked to other successful tech companies, such as Amazon, for practices that he could emulate. One that he liked was developing a set of company values. In doing so at Uber, he created a set of values that were unique in content and style. In general, he emphasized the need for what he called the mind-set of a champion. This starts with a complete commitment to one's business and work. He told a group of students,

> Fall in love with an idea. Just go after it. When you do that, win or lose, . . . it is a worthwhile endeavor. . . . If you've got love, it's much easier than if you don't. . . . The entrepreneur that loves what they are doing going against the entrepreneur who doesn't, [it's] really obvious who wins that one. Not even a close call.[19]

In Kalanick's management philosophy a champion puts everything he or she has into making the business a success—"leaving everything on the field." He said that those building a firm need to push forward and have no doubts about their ability to succeed, noting that, "Fear is disease, hustle is the antidote, . . . crazy hustle, grit your teeth, claw your way to success, no easy way to do it."[20] Kalanick saw himself as having an ability to work his way through adversity. The movie *Pulp Fiction* has a character named Winston Wolfe, who is called on to deal with difficult situations. In the film, one of Wolfe's associates kills someone and Wolfe is called to dispose of the body, along with the car in which the killing took place. Kalanick reportedly saw himself as a fixer, like the movie character, capable of managing chaotic and stressful situations that would overwhelm most people.[21]

Kalanick also believes in embracing conflict when it serves a productive purpose—what he calls "principled confrontation."[22] He believes in challenging ideas, people, institutions, and laws that are, in his mind, on the wrong side of progress. He viewed taxi companies and regulatory agencies as stuck in the past, failing to provide innovative technologies and approaches that would improve public transportation. Worse, he saw them as corrupt in putting their own financial and political interests above the interests of customers—in part, by blocking firms such as Uber from operating in their municipalities.

One example was Miami-Dade County, which had regulations forcing riders to book a car service at least sixty minutes in advance and pay no less than eighty dollars for each ride. Kalanick, intentionally or not, became a champion for those fighting against governmental interference in the spread of technological innovations. When asked about San Francisco's aggressive response to his company, he noted, "We're totally legal, like totally legal, and the government is telling us to shut down. And you can either do what they say, or you can fight for what you believe."[23] Kalanick saw each city as a battleground that needed to be won by an aggressive campaign, and Uber team, that would force special interest groups to cave under public pressure. To that end, he wanted a company of people who shared his core belief in principled confrontation. One person who applied for a job at the firm recalled, "I did an interview there this year, and it was the most aggressive questioning I've ever had. . . . Nothing compared to the 'cultural' interview where [they] gave me an example of knowingly breaking the law because 'they knew they were right' and then asked if I had a similar work experience I could describe."[24]

To Kalanick, rebelling against the status quo was a business imperative for Uber and a moral obligation. His mentality was that of an insurgent fighting against what he perceived to be a corrupt institution. Someone who knows him states, "He really thrives when he can subvert the norm."[25] Eric Schmidt, former executive chairman of Alphabet, noted that Kalanick "is the definition of a serial entrepreneur in its purest form, with all the strengths and weaknesses that comes with it. He's a fighter. . . . He can be disagreeable in that sense that, well, he disagrees."[26] An investor in Uber put it more bluntly, maintaining that, "It's hard to be a disrupter and not be an asshole."[27]

MISTAKES, MISDEEDS & SCANDALS

Kalanick was relentless in his pursuit of growth. The problem was that his obsession too often blinded him to other considerations. To be fair, he was passionate about finding the most efficient way to move people from one point to another. The mathematician in him viewed this as a problem worthy of his intellect, and he was tenacious in his efforts to improve Uber's ability to match supply with demand in cities around the world.[28] However, his words and actions suggest that beating his adversaries in the pursuit of growth was his primary goal. Mark Cuban, who had invested in Red Swoosh, knew Kalanick well and was afraid that his desire to win battles was more important than building a service that people found indispensable.

Kalanick had difficulty recognizing when his overwhelming drive became counterproductive. Too often, his behavior and that of his firm violated social, ethical, and potentially legal boundaries. Some of his transgressions were of a public relations variety in saying things that damaged his reputation and his company's brand. Other actions, particularly regarding Uber's company culture and marketplace behavior, were even more damaging. Consider that:

- Kalanick alienated regulators and politicians with his aggressive approach to overcoming those who he viewed as protecting the taxi industry. He told an industry group that Uber was engaged in a political battle where "the candidate is Uber and the opponent is an asshole named Taxi. Nobody likes him, he's not a nice character, but he's so woven into the political machinery and fabric that a lot of people owe him favors."[29] Kalanick was no less aggressive in his public pronouncements regarding his competitors, such as Lyft (whom he described as a clone of Uber and not worth talking about), as well as customers who found fault with Uber's practices. In one interview, he described those who criticized Uber's surge pricing as not being smart enough to understand the economic laws of supply and demand.

- The company used covert software to avoid detection by municipalities striving to limit access of Uber cars in certain areas of their cities (such as airports). Uber placed a bogus version of their app on the phones of those suspected of being government regulators, preventing them from monitoring the true location of Uber's cars. Once installed, the software disguised the cars' locations with the intent of showing, falsely, that drivers were not working in the off-limit areas.

- Uber hid from Apple that it was secretly identifying and tagging iPhones. Uber was dealing with account fraud—iPhones stolen in Asia were being used by unethical drivers to set up fake accounts and then book fake rides. Uber was then paying financial rewards to drivers based on these fraudulent bookings.[30] The company's solution was embedding an identifying code, called a fingerprint, in each iPhone, which would remain even after the user erased the phone. The hidden code allowed Uber to stop the fraudulent use of stolen phones. However, Apple has a clear policy that its phones, once erased, will leave no trace of the previous owner's identity. Uber knew this and sought to avoid detection by Apple through what is called "geofencing," a software that allowed Uber to hide its secret code. Apple eventually uncovered Uber's deception, and its CEO, Tim Cook, informed Kalanick that if Uber didn't stop, Apple would bar its app from its phones.
- For a full year, Uber failed to disclose a data hack that compromised the confidential information of fifty-seven million driver and rider accounts. Uber identified the two hackers and paid them one hundred thousand dollars to destroy the data and not go public with the breach. The company reported the payout as one in which they paid the hackers to attack their software as a preventative measure (what is sometimes called a "bug bounty"). Once this became known, users and the press accused Uber of paying a ransom to criminals to keep the hack secret in an attempt to avoid negative fallout with customers and investors. The general sentiment was that, at the very least, Uber was irresponsible in not telling riders and drivers that their personal data had been stolen by a third party via a data breach.[31]
- Uber was alleged to have received confidential documents regarding autonomous car technology, which were taken from

a competitor. Alphabet's Waymo unit filed a lawsuit against Uber claiming that a former Waymo executive, Anthony Levandowski, downloaded fourteen thousand confidential files and, in doing so, stole intellectual property related to the firm's work on autonomous car technology. Waymo and Uber settled the court case, with Uber paying Alphabet an estimated $245 million in damages.[32]

- Uber started testing autonomous cars in San Francisco without obtaining necessary permits from the state of California. Uber didn't think its technology-enabled cars met the definition of an autonomous vehicle, as they were under the supervision of a driver. Videotapes of Uber vehicles, some allegedly running red lights, were made public and the state closed down the operation. Some people speculated that Uber failed to register the cars because they would need to report any situations in which the driver took control of the car as well as any infractions (such as running red lights).[33]

- The toxic aspects of Uber's culture became highly visible when Susan Fowler, an engineer who worked for the company for one year, published a blog post that described a corporate environment that was hostile to women and unwilling to act on her claims of being sexually harassed by her supervisor.[34] When Fowler's blog went viral, other employees went public with similar claims, including harassment by supervisors and colleagues if the employees reported discriminatory practices and behaviors. Under public pressure, Uber conducted internal and external investigations of its workplace environment, including following up on more than two hundred complaints made by employees to human resources. The result of the inquiry was the termination of twenty Uber employees and numerous changes in the company's management policies and practices. These changes included

reviewing the firm's compensation practices to address
potential gender bias and appointing a Chief Operating
Officer to overcome more general deficiencies in operations.[35]

Kalanick faced an onslaught of problems: vacancies in critical
executive roles, increasingly negative stories in the press, strikes by
drivers protesting the company's compensation policies, protests by
taxi industry groups, legal actions by regulators and competitors, and
charges of an out-of-control "bro-culture" that discriminated against
women. Admitting his part in the problems, Kalanick said, "I realize
that I can come off as a somewhat fierce advocate for Uber. I also realize
that some have used a different 'A' word to describe me. . . . Well, I'll
be the first to admit that I'm not perfect and neither is this company.
Like everyone else, we make mistakes."[36]

His public apology, however, was not enough for his firm's largest
shareholders. Early investors Mitch and Freada Kapor wrote an open
letter that stated, "Uber has been here many times before, responding
to public exposure of bad behavior by holding an all-hands meeting,
apologizing and vowing to change, only to quickly return to aggressive
business as usual." Some of the institutional shareholders were worried
that the company was facing an unmanageable barrage of negative
publicity that would persist as long as Kalanick remained CEO. He
had come to personify what was wrong with Uber. The value of their
investments, now worth billions of dollars, was at risk of being eroded
before the payout of an anticipated initial public offering.

A group of institutional investors, led by the venture capital firm
Benchmark, called for Kalanick to resign as CEO.[37] They stated
that he had become a liability and new leadership was needed. One
board member said, "We reached a point where we felt like the entire
company and all of its constituencies—drivers, riders, employees,
shareholders—were at risk if the company continued to move in the
direction it was."[38]

At the same time, Kalanick suffered a family tragedy when a boating accident resulted in the death of his mother and serious injuries to his father. One month later, Kalanick resigned as CEO. He wrote on his departure, "I love Uber more than anything in the world and at this difficult moment in my personal life, I have accepted the investors request to step aside, so that Uber can go back to building rather than be distracted with another fight."[39]

Uber's new leader, Dara Khosrowshahi, praised Kalanick for building an exceptional company. At the same time, he faulted the company, and by default Kalanick, for being "willing to make trade-offs related to how we did business, and I think was guilty of hubris, was guilty of thinking they knew better than others." He added, "What we know now clearly is that breakneck growth can hide cultural issues. There are no excuses for not doing the right thing."[40]

HERO, VILLAIN, OR BOTH?

A "fundamental attribution error" occurs when we give more credit, or blame, to an individual than he or she deserves for a particular outcome. It is an error because larger forces are typically at play in determining how events unfold in a company or society. Focusing on an individual's role simplifies a complex world by suggesting that one person is responsible for a broader set of dynamics that we don't fully understand. Consider the extraordinary success of the film company Pixar after it was bought by Steve Jobs. Pixar revolutionized the animated film industry with technically innovative and critically acclaimed movies. Jobs had a positive influence on Pixar's success, in terms of the money he invested and his management influence. However, it is equally true that co-leaders Ed Catmull and John Lasseter played pivotal roles in the firm's ability to produce one blockbuster after another. Who was most important in making Pixar what it is today?

Jobs was the most visible leader of the three, given his previous fame at Apple, and received much of the credit—but it's likely that all three were essential to the firm's success.[41]

In the case of Uber, we run that risk of attributing both its successes and failures solely to Travis Kalanick. We shouldn't minimize the impact of his leadership, but we need to consider a broader set of factors when seeking to understand the Uber story and what we can learn from it. That said, any assessment of Uber begins with Kalanick's influence on the firm. On the positive front, Uber is a company worthy of our attention because of Kalanick's leadership. Camp developed the groundbreaking ride-sharing technology, but it was Kalanick who shaped the firm's growth strategy and business operations. One wonders if any leader other than Kalanick could have created a company that grew at the incredible rate it did during his tenure. He possessed a unique set of skills that resulted in a nearly perfect match for what Uber needed early in its history. He is gifted at analysis, creative in solving complex problems, skilled at raising capital, and able to execute at a high level. Garrett Camp, the firm's founder, was right to view Kalanick as the person he needed to drive the growth of the company. One observer noted,

> Disruption is never easy and many who try fail. To upend the transportation industry with his ride-sharing app, Kalanick shrugged off legal threats, ignored taxi protests, and sent Uber crashing through regulatory barriers. . . . He was never willing to negotiate, even with the people making the rules, if their solution didn't fit his vision to make calling an Uber car the easiest way to get around town.[42]

Few people have built a company with the meteoric growth of Uber. It makes life better for millions of people each day. It is also the model on which a host of "on-demand" services, such as grocery delivery, are changing how we live. A company board member, who was among those calling for Kalanick to resign, still recognized what Travis Kalanick had achieved. He wrote, "There will be many pages in the history books devoted to @travisk—very few entrepreneurs have had such a lasting impact on the world."[43] A petition was circulated within the company to bring Kalanick back after he resigned, with over a thousand people signing it. One Uber employee wrote a defense of Kalanick on Facebook, saying he inspired people to "think bigger, faster, and higher impact than anyone has ever dared to think before."[44] His supporters admitted that he made mistakes but said they were the result, in part, of Uber facing obstacles that required a more aggressive, no-holds-barred, approach. Chris Messina, Uber's former developer experience lead, says that we should judge Kalanick in the context of the transportation industry. "The environment that Uber plays in has many more vested interests who operate by a different set of rules" compared to previous Silicon Valley success stories, Messina says. "So then, is it appropriate to use the same rubrics to evaluate Travis and the culture he's created? Are we really comparing apples to apples?"[45]

Others believe Uber's rapid growth, and decentralized organizational structure, resulted in a chaotic environment where mistakes were likely. The company was expanding at a rate few firms have ever experienced and lacked the culture, practices, and talent needed to prevent misdeeds. Marisa Mayer, who was a senior executive at Google and then CEO of Yahoo, defended Kalanick, saying she believed he was unaware of the transgressions taking place (particularly concerning charges of discrimination). She noted, "Scale is incredibly tricky . . . I think he's a phenomenal leader; Uber is ridiculously interesting . . . I just don't think he knew. When your company scales that quickly, it's hard."[46]

Kalanick, however, was the person driving growth, and thus he bears responsibility for not managing the risks associated with what he created. More directly, he was the source of many of the problems.

Executives in Silicon Valley often talk about the challenge of scaling a firm—by which they mean developing the formal and informal processes needed to manage an increasingly large company. Leaders are continually fighting a battle between promoting growth and managing the resulting chaos. That certainly was the case at Uber, which is understandable but not an excuse for what occurred. The problem, in part, was Kalanick's failure to scale as a leader. He demonstrated all of the strengths and limitations that were apparent in his earlier leadership roles, but now he was in a much larger firm—one with more impact and visibility. Three of his leadership missteps are particularly noteworthy for those seeking to learn from his experience:

Tone-Deaf: At times Kalanick lacked the emotional and social intelligence that we expect from the leaders of prominent companies. The press praised him for being a new type of leader, one who would do what others feared to do and express what others dared not to say. Compared to most image-conscious corporate leaders, whose public statements are typically cautious and politically correct, Kalanick was unapologetically honest about his beliefs and tactics. But the problem was that he went too far and made statements that came back to hurt him and his company.

During one public forum he answered a question regarding the future of autonomous cars. He said they were inevitable for two reasons. First, they would be safer. One million people a year are killed in car accidents, and autonomous cars will be a safer form of transportation. A second factor that would drive their growth was cost. Expenses would decline because the "other dude in the car," the driver, was expensive. Get rid of the driver and you save money. Kalanick's statement, while accurate, was not well received by the thousands of drivers who were working hard to provide daily service to Uber's customers.[47]

Another example of Kalanick failing to understand the impact of his words occurred when an interviewer asked if his life had changed as a result of Uber's success. Kalanick said he sometimes refers to the company as "boober" because women found him more attractive as the leader of a highly successful company. This statement didn't sit well with many of his customers. A third well-publicized example of Kalanick's lack of emotional intelligence is the memo he sent to his employees before a company retreat in Miami. In it, he describes what he expects of his colleagues, outlining the CEO dos ("Have a great fucking time") and don'ts ("Do not have sex with another employee *UNLESS* a) you have asked that person for that privilege and they have responded with an emphatic '*YES!* I will have sex with you' *AND* b) the two [or more] of you do not work in the same chain of command. Yes, that means that Travis will be celibate on this trip."[48] The memo was leaked to the press and resulted in predictably negative headlines.

Ethically Challenged:[49] A second, even more fatal, flaw was Kalanick's win-at-all-costs mentality. Those who build visionary companies are often tough individuals who do what is needed for their firms to survive and prosper. He was more extreme—with a history of operating close to the line regarding ethical and legal violations. Early in Kalanick's career, media companies sued Scour for allowing what was claimed to be illegal downloads of music and movies. Later, Red Swoosh inappropriately used its employee tax withholdings for general business purposes. Uber faced accusations because of Kalanick acting inappropriately toward employees, drivers, customers, and competitors. In some respects, he is similar to Jeff Skilling, another hyperaggressive CEO who was the president of the energy company Enron. Skilling went to jail for crimes that included fraud and insider trading. As noted earlier, Kalanick was not convicted of any illegal activities. But his actions suggest that he was similar to Skilling in promoting his company's growth above all else. One commentator noted that "Uber embodied Silicon Valley's capitalist id—unrepentant about winning at all costs."[50]

Great leaders, like great athletes, are not always admirable people. The traits that give rise to their remarkable achievements can also result in questionable actions. It is naïve to assume that greatness in one area of a person's life results in commendable qualities in other areas. The best leaders produce products and services that benefit society—but may do so in a manner that is unappealing and even, to an extent, damaging. That was true of Kalanick, whose aggressive approach both served and undermined Uber. He is not unique. Steve Jobs acted at times in a deceitful and punishing manner toward both colleagues and those outside of Apple who questioned his actions. Part of the reason Elon Musk lost early leadership roles in companies he founded was his harsh treatment of those who worked for him. The question is, At what point does a leader's actions cross a line and cause more harm than good? What are the ethical boundaries that can't be crossed? At what point do they become so damaged in the eyes of stakeholders, such as customers, employees, and shareholders, that they can't recover and continue to lead?

Obsessive leaders need people around them who can protect them from themselves. Having a group of advisors is particularly important when a leader pushes his or her strengths to the extreme, risking those strengths becoming weaknesses. It appears that Kalanick was surrounded by people who thought alike in being unrelenting advocates for growth. They were too much like Kalanick, or lacked the authority to prevent the scandals that ultimately plagued the company. Kalanick's key operational, human-resources, and legal leaders particularly bear some responsibility for not preventing the missteps that engulfed Uber during the final years of Kalanick's tenure. Challenging one's boss is never easy, but it does occur in a well-functioning team. At Uber, it appears that no one could rein in Kalanick. The president of the company, Jeff Jones, resigned only six months after joining Uber. He stated on his departure, "It is now clear, however, that the beliefs and approach to leadership that have guided my career are inconsistent with what I saw and experienced at Uber, and I can no longer continue as president of the ride-sharing business."[51]

Collapsing Narrative: Kalanick's third leadership mistake was failing to control the story that evolved about him and his company. Early in the firm's history, the media lauded him for brashly creating a ride-sharing service that people loved. His style was also attractive as a CEO of an important company who talked like a Southern California surfer. In one interview he described how a Woody Allen movie, made when the director was in his seventies, inspired Kalanick after the disappointments of his first start-ups: "I'm like, that dude is old. And he is still bringing it! . . . And I'm like, all right, I've got a chance, man. I can do it."[52] In another speech he described the Uber software created by company founder Garrett Camp: "I am living in the future. I pushed a button and a car rolled up and now I'm a frickin' pimp. Garret is the guy who invented that shit."[53] This is not the way the CEOs of most billion-dollar corporations talk—and some found that appealing. Anand Sanwal noted how many in the news media as well as the general public viewed the company positively in its early years:

> Uber's narrative was super compelling. Brash founder takes on entrenched slow-moving industry, changes the game, and creates a massively valuable service that folks liked. . . . And he was doing it while also raising a middle finger at regulatory bodies and competitors.[54]

Sentiment, however, turned on Kalanick—with the media and public finding fault with his words, actions, and the culture he created at Uber. The company went from being a scrappy start-up committed to improving peoples' lives, to being seen as playing dirty in its desire to win at all costs. The fact that Uber had provided more than ten billion rides over its history was lost in a maze of bad publicity.[55] One event that contributed to the shift in view occurred when Kalanick was caught on video in the back of an Uber black car discussing compensation policies that the driver, a man named Fawzi, disliked.

Fawzi thought Uber wasn't paying its drivers enough. At one point Kalanick responded, "Some people don't like to take responsibility for their own shit. They blame everything in their life on somebody else. Good luck." Why the driver videotaped the exchange with Kalanick and then posted it on the internet can be debated (with some suggesting that this was not a chance occurrence).[56] The fallout from the video portrayed Kalanick as a wealthy CEO who didn't care about the people working on the front lines of his company. The video resulted in a rare public apology from Kalanick via a memo to his colleagues:

> By now I'm sure you've seen the video where I treated an Uber driver disrespectfully. To say that I am ashamed is an extreme understatement. My job as your leader is to lead . . . and that starts with behaving in a way that makes us all proud. That is not what I did, and it cannot be explained away. It's clear this video is a reflection of me—and the criticism we've received is a stark reminder that I must fundamentally change as a leader and grow up. This is the first time I've been willing to admit that I need leadership help and I intend to get it. I want to profoundly apologize to Fawzi, as well as the driver and rider community, and to the Uber team.[57]

Another incident is noteworthy. One of Kalanick's senior executives, Emil Michael, said that Uber was willing to spend a great deal of money, upwards of $1 million, to conduct investigative research on journalists who wrote stories about the company that it felt were unfair. One journalist, Sarah Lacy, was signaled out by Michael as a target for such an investigation. Her articles described what she saw as Uber's misogyny, telling her readers that she had removed the firm's app from her phone.[58] Lacy appropriately took Michael's words as a threat with the intent of damaging her reputation and stopping her from writing articles that Uber didn't like. We can only assume that other journalists were angry at the intimidation directed at one of their own and what they saw as an attack on the freedom of the press. Once the account of Michael's comments went public, he apologized and said that his words were off-the-record and did not represent what he and Uber truly believe.[59] It is safe to assume that most in the media didn't accept his apology.

Kalanick also alienated customers, as a result of Uber's approach, which some saw as taking advantage of them in a time of need. Kalanick countered that other industries, such as airlines and hotels, used the same approach. In the case of Uber, higher prices at peak periods of demand resulted in more drivers on the road, which meant faster pickup times and better service. Surge pricing, however, was poorly communicated. Riders didn't appreciate being charged much higher fares during a snowstorm or taxi strike. Uber notified riders before a pickup that peak pricing was in effect and there was a higher estimated fare. However, that didn't alter the negative perception of Uber's surge practices. Kalanick was quickly becoming typecast as a greedy and callous CEO who didn't care about his customers, and in doing so gave his opponents reasons to portray him as an unethical leader.[60]

Other leaders have faced similar—although less extreme—criticisms. But some, such as Bezos, understand the impact of a company's public persona. According to author Brad Stone, several years ago Bezos engaged his leadership team in a discussion about the importance of a company being seen in a favorable light by the public. In a memo to his team called "amazon.love," he questioned why some firms have a positive public image (such as Apple) and others don't (such as Goldman Sachs). Bezos stated that sustaining a positive reputation was critical to public support for a firm's long-term growth, and he outlined seventeen attributes that he believed contributed to a company's positive reputation. Uber passed the test on some of the characteristics for being what Bezos called "cool" (being innovative and exploratory) but failed on others (being rude and obsessing over competitors).[61]

The key difference is that Bezos does not believe Amazon's goal is to be disruptive—the company's goal is to delight customers. However, Bezos and Amazon are now facing some of the same criticisms that were leveled at Kalanick and Uber. A recent *New Yorker* article described Bezos as the "master of cutthroat capitalism." His desire for "amazon.love" is being severely tested by those who find fault with the firm's competitive practices and impact on society. Amazon faces criticism across a range of issues including, but not limited to, potential antitrust violations as the firm grows increasingly large, the threat his company poses to traditional retail stores and employment, a reportedly low level of corporate federal taxation, the demanding working conditions in the firm's fulfillment centers, the authenticity and safety of its products, and the company's historic resistance to unionization. The sentiment regarding Amazon has become increasingly negative, and Bezos needs to be careful that being relentless isn't viewed by the public as being ruthless.[62]

THE TRUST IMPERATIVE

The cumulative effect of Kalanick's mistakes meant that many of his key stakeholders no longer trusted him.[63] The first imperative in sustaining trust is that a leader needs to deliver results. On most counts Kalanick's ability in this area was extraordinary. Ridership increased each year and investors were competing to pour money into the firm at an ever-increasing valuation. There were problems, such as an inability to establish itself in China; however, in most of its markets, Uber continued to attract riders at a rapid rate. The second trust imperative is to act with integrity. Kalanick largely failed in this regard given the scandals that plagued the company. Third, a leader needs to demonstrate concern for others, particularly customers and employees. This requires empathy to see the world from their point of view. Again, Kalanick's words and actions made him appear self-serving and callous. He created a service that people loved, but his actions suggested he was more focused on his company's growth and profitability than the well-being of customers, colleagues, and drivers.

Trust is earned when all three imperatives—results, integrity, and concern—are evident. Kalanick delivered results, and that allowed some, particularly shareholders, to be more tolerant of his objectionable behavior. But his ongoing missteps eroded perceptions of his integrity and concern for others. There is a threshold that, once crossed, results in broken trust. Kalanick crossed both integrity and concern thresholds and couldn't find his way back.

At times Kalanick talked about Uber as being his spouse—whom he loved more than anything in the world.[64] This level of commitment can result in defensive behavior when a leader feels that his or her company is under threat. Combine this with the confidence that comes with great success, and the result can be a leader closed to feedback and advice. Kalanick was the driving force in bringing to life a company that faced daunting obstacles. He encountered entrenched opposition in the transportation industry and government, who tried to kill his company. Kalanick made mistakes but we can understand why he didn't change his approach, given the extraordinary level of success he achieved at Uber and the need to fight those who opposed him. He eventually realized he was at risk if he didn't mature as a leader, but that realization came too late.

He had lost the trust of his key investors, the media, many of his drivers, and some of his customers. His leadership failure, all told, was failing to grow at the pace needed to manage an increasingly complex and important company.

Kalanick is not alone in being responsible for the crisis at Uber. The larger governance system at the company was equally guilty. In particular, Uber's board failed to monitor and temper Kalanick's worst instincts. His board members were not naïve about his temperament. I suspect that they were leery of repeating the mistake made over thirty years earlier, when Apple's board pushed Steve Jobs out of the company he founded. The fear of firing a visionary founder can result in a board that is largely passive or, in more extreme cases, serves as "enablers and apologists."[65]

This tendency is compounded by the structure of many boards, particularly in the tech industry, where the founders retain authority of their firms. Entrepreneurs often want to structure their companies in a manner where they maintain control via voting stock after their firm goes public. The result can be board members and shareholders who have limited power in forcing changes in a leader's behavior, or the practices and culture of a company.[66] In the case of Uber, Travis Kalanick, Garrett Camp, and Ryan Graves (the firm's first CEO and then general manager) retained voting control of the company, which meant that Uber's board members and primary shareholders could offer advice—but only advice unless the three principals supported their proposals.

Some investment firms are also guilty of enabling dysfunctional leader behavior because they strive to position themselves as "founder-friendly." These firms want start-up founders to consider them for early-stage investments, for obvious reasons. Investment firms with a history of removing founders are generally not looked upon favorably by other entrepreneurs. Founders have reason to be concerned, since research indicates that a majority of them eventually step down from leadership roles in their firms—with four out of five being forced to do so by investors or board members.[67] The passivity of boards and investors is even more likely when the founder has created something exceptional—and, in the case of Uber, is producing billions of dollars in capital gains for its shareholders. All told, removing a founder or controlling his or her behavior is not an easy task. This was noted by board member Bill Gurley, who remarked on Kalanick's resignation, "Everything that happened this summer was a very difficult decision for us. . . . The two questions we get most often are, 'How could you possibly have done this?' and 'Why didn't you do it sooner?' Obviously, those are in stark contrast with one another."[68]

Uber's board member with the most accountability for Uber's mistakes, other than Kalanick, is Garrett Camp. As the firm's cofounder, at times chairman, and one of its largest shareholders, he was the one person who had the formal and informal power to influence Kalanick. In the absence of a powerful board, it fell to Camp to play a productive role in protecting Uber from Kalanick's obsessive downsides. Camp had wanted a pit bull and Kalanick played the role expected of him. But when a dog bites someone, do you blame the dog? Personality in many respects is "hard-wired" and based on what happened at Uber, Kalanick's temperament proved to be only somewhat malleable. Camp needed to act as a counterbalancing force.

We don't know what conversations occurred between the two, but we do know the outcome given the company's wrongdoings. Camp was either unaware of what was happening in the company or didn't intervene in a sufficiently forceful manner. In either case, he was at fault. After Kalanick resigned, Camp said that Uber had been experiencing growing pains and failed to build the systems and culture needed to operate effectively as its ridership increased. He believed the company had learned from its mistakes and would listen more carefully to the people who enabled its growth—in particular, Uber's team members and drivers. Camp did not directly criticize Kalanick or take accountability for his role in Uber's shortcomings. Instead, he focused on the future and Uber's positive impact on society.

The media also bears some responsibility for what happened at Uber by portraying Kalanick first as a hero and then as a villain. He was initially held up as the model for a new breed of CEOs—young, brilliant, and confrontational. He morphed into a greedy capitalist who acted in antisocial ways. In the end, the media made sure that Kalanick couldn't escape from the damning narrative that he helped create through his irresponsible words and actions. He became the target for a broader set of concerns about how large technology firms were failing to act responsibly. One tech journalist, observing the negative slant on anything involving Kalanick, tweeted, "He's not the monster the media turned him into."[69] Those with a conspiratorial mentality go further and suggest that some targeted Kalanick because he challenged powerful interest groups, such as taxi and limo authorities and their political supporters. They warned that other visionary leaders, including Elon Musk, will face the same risk if their firms grow and threaten dominant interests in their respective industries.

The lesson of Kalanick is that obsessive leaders and teams are always at risk of being so focused on their goal and so passionate about protecting their firms that they self-destruct. Travis Kalanick's single-minded quest to make Uber the dominant company in the transportation industry hurt the company he loved and ended his tenure as CEO. His fixation with getting people and products from point A to B as fast as possible was the same mind-set he applied to the growth of his company. He played to the hilt his part in the Uber story—fulfilling the only role he knew how to play. His rise and fall, perhaps more than any recent business leader, illustrates why obsession is at once a blessing and a curse.

TAKEAWAYS

- Travis Kalanick was willing to do what was needed to make Uber into what it is today. He was the force behind Uber establishing ridesharing as a viable transportation alternative and the model that other firms copied in markets around the world.
- He let his obsession with "juicing growth" take priority over doing what was right. The result was a series of missteps and scandals that threatened to undermine what Kalanick and his team had built.
- His demise was due, in part, to having no one to prevent his self-destructive acts—no one on his board, executive team, or group of advisors who could protect him from the downsides of his obsessive nature.

MAKING
OBSESSION
WORK

6

THE INDIVIDUAL'S CHOICE:
ALL IN OR NOT?

Whenever anything is being accomplished,
it is being done, I have learned,
by a monomaniac with a mission.
                                    —Peter Drucker[1]

Professors J. Stuart Bunderson and Jeffery Thompson are experts in the psychology of deeply meaningful work. Ten years ago they conducted a study that focused on a single profession, one they believed would provide insights into the pros and cons of being occupationally consumed. Their choice of professions? Zookeepers. As a group, zookeepers have high levels of motivation even though their pay is relatively low, putting them in the bottom quartile of compensation for those with college degrees. Their commitment is even more striking when considering the undesirable aspects of their work.

Zookeepers work among wild animals that can injure or kill them at any given moment. Constant vigilance is needed to protect themselves as well as their fellow zookeepers. They also face the unpleasant task of cleaning zoo enclosures in the rain, cold, and heat, including the daily removal of animal feces. Many zookeepers, as well, are on call outside of their regular work hours and required to come to work if the animals under their care need attention at any time of the day or night. But the danger, drudgery, and obligations don't deter those who want to work in a zoo. Many serve as unpaid interns before being offered permanent positions. Even then, they have little opportunity to advance because most zoos have limited supervisory positions, tight budgets, and low turnover. The question, then, is why zookeepers are so highly motivated.[2]

The easy answer is that their love of animals allows them to tolerate the demands of their profession. The researchers found, however, that something deeper was going on. After surveying close to a thousand individuals in hundreds of zoos, they concluded that many zookeepers believe that they are destined to work with animals and have a duty to ensure their survival regardless of the personal sacrifices involved. They love animals, as do many people, but their career choice was not based primarily on personal desires or the pursuit of individual fulfillment. Instead, zookeepers feel they are personally called to protect animals and save them from extinction. The researchers noted that, "There was this idea that they were born to do this work. . . . Working as a zookeeper felt like a personal destiny to many of them. They even shared stories about how events led them to the zoo, as if by fate."[3] The researchers summarized their findings in an article titled "The Call of the Wild."

The other conclusion from the study is that vocation, at least for zookeepers, extracts a toll. Those with the greatest sense of calling were more likely to sacrifice for the job—be it lower pay, less personal time, or physical hardships. In other words, the more dedicated the zookeeper, the more likely he or she will pay the price for being so.

A sense of calling complicates the relationship between zookeepers and their work, fostering a sense of occupational identification, transcendent meaning, and occupational importance, on the one hand, and unbending duty, personal sacrifice, and heightened vigilance, on the other. Our investigations among this sample of zookeepers therefore suggest that a calling can be a painfully double-edged sword.[4]

Going further, another line of research suggests that those who are passionate about their work are more likely to be taken advantage of by supervisors and organizations.[5] This may involve employees being asked to work longer, do more, and perform work outside of their job description. These demands occur because others believe that passionate individuals find their work intrinsically motivating and would volunteer to do the extra work when others would not. The researchers conclude that passion, while having many benefits, has a downside—what they call "passion exploitation."

VOCATION—FOUND OR CREATED?

The definition of vocation is "a summons or strong inclination to a particular state or course of action."[6] Its origin is the Latin word *vocare*, which means "to call" and originally designated those who entered a religious order. Vocation is the close sibling of obsession, with the latter suggesting possession and the former implying calling. In both cases, the individual is under the influence of a force that drives him or her to pursue something of central importance.

The meaning of vocation expanded through the writings of Martin Luther and John Calvin. They proposed that each person could manifest God's will by producing something beneficial to humankind through work, including activities as mundane as baking bread or making shoes. They further maintained that each person, regardless of his or her status in society, was called to contribute to human welfare through their work. Work thus becomes more than a means to put food on the table and shelter over one's head—it is a divine act with moral and social implications.[7]

From this viewpoint, the vocational mandate is to find and live out one's calling. The more extreme version of this belief suggests that people are vehicles for forces greater than themselves. Jeff Bezos made this point when he said, "You don't choose your passions; your passions choose you. How they're formed, you're not completely sure. But I do think you get imprinted somehow early on with certain things, you just get excited about them."[8] Bezos added that, "Many, many kids and many grown-ups do figure out over time what their passions are. . . . I don't think it's that hard. I think what happens, though, sometimes, is that we let our intellectual selves overrule those passions—and so that's what needs to be guarded against.[9] The goal, then, is to uncover what already exists and become the person you are destined to be.

An example of uncovering one's calling is the musician Mark Knopfler of Dire Straits fame. At the age of eighteen months he would sit with his mother and listen to songs on the radio and his mother's voice as she sang along. At the age of six he recalls thinking "music is for me" and feeling that his path in life was clear. At age fifteen his father bought him his first electric guitar—which he later described as the best day of his childhood. In college, Knopfler majored in English and began to write songs. He joined a band soon after graduating and has now spent almost fifty years in the industry, performing and producing music.[10]

A second way of viewing vocation, best articulated by Professor Carol Dweck of Stanford University, is that vocation arises over time as a result of experience, mainly through trial and error.[11] Dweck maintains that the goal is not to uncover your calling but to actively create it through effort and exploration. Vocation, then, is not found but made. The difference may be subtle, but those who support a developmental approach to vocation argue that it is important. Entrepreneur Kent Healy emphasizes this: "Searching for your passion is not proactive; it's actually quite passive, because embedded in the pursuit is the erroneous belief that when seen, it will be immediately recognized. The reality is that one's lifelong passion is often revealed through working passionately on something you have immediate access to."[12] Most individuals don't uncover their calling at age six or follow a straight or smooth path in their career. In other words, those who are "called" are a rarity.

Instead, people try a variety of things before settling on an occupational choice that, ideally, will consume them for years if not decades. One of the researchers of the "develop your passion" approach noted,

> If you look at something and think, "that seems inter-esting, that could be an area I could make a contribution in," you then invest yourself in it. . . . You take some time to do it, you encounter challenges, over time you build that commitment.[13]

Consider Brian Chesky, cofounder of the well-known house-sharing company Airbnb. He studied design in college and worked in several industrial-design roles post graduation. After several years in what he said were uninspiring jobs, he moved to San Francisco with the idea of becoming an entrepreneur. He wasn't sure what business he would pursue and experimented with several ventures—including marketing cereal boxes with political figures on the front.[14] During this period, Chesky and a friend also created a website offering overnight stays in their San Francisco apartment (with the first guests sleeping on an air mattress). They soon realized that some people wanted to experience the sense of belonging that comes with sharing a home with a friendly host versus staying in a more impersonal hotel. Chesky saw a business opportunity and with two partners built a company that would arrange such experiences, using technology to bring together hosts and guests. As Airbnb grew, he came to believe that his calling was to foster a sense of belonging—first among his firm's guests and hosts but also among his colleagues and within the communities in which they work. His title is now CEO and Head of Community at Airbnb, a company that has hosted 500 million people since its founding just over ten years ago.[15] If you asked Chesky as a teenager about his future occupation, I doubt he would have said his calling was to create communities of belonging around the world.

Dweck maintains that those who embrace a fixed notion of vocation, thinking that their calling only needs to be uncovered, hurt their chances of being successful in their search. A fixed notion of vocation can result in people turning away from potential areas of meaningful work because they don't find it immediately fascinating. They close off opportunities that require more time to be fully explored and, if appropriate, embraced. In the absence of an immediate connection, they assume that the work must not be their calling. They may also walk away from a potential vocation when the work becomes challenging or frustrating—thinking, erroneously, that a vocational calling is always pleasurable and highly motivating. Dweck presents a contrary view in suggesting that one's calling evolves with experience, as people "grow to fit their vocations better over time."[16]

Several factors are apparent in those with a strong sense of vocation, be it found or created. First, their calling is endlessly fascinating to them. They care about their work and can spend a vast amount of time on it, when others would become bored and move on to something else. They believe their "work is much more fun than fun."[17] Steve Jobs told college students in a now-famous commencement speech that "your work is going to fill a large part of your life, and the only way to be truly satisfied is to do what you believe is great work. And the only way to do great work is to love what you do. If you haven't found it yet, keep looking. Don't settle."[18] One reason this is important is that achievement in any profession takes years of effort, and passion provides the motivation to push forward when others might quit. This includes engaging in what researchers call "deliberate practice."[19] These are the elements of one's vocation that require more work for the individual to reach a higher level of performance. Vocational passion can result in doing what is required to excel by focusing on the areas in which one needs to improve.

We can also assume that a strong sense of vocation is more likely when the individual has a natural ability in his or her area of interest.

Talent, beyond its obvious benefits, can increase a person's drive to achieve a goal. Most people enjoy engaging in activities at which they excel and are motivated by the recognition they receive for doing so. Someone with natural ability will most likely put more time and energy into a task and be more likely to succeed over time. Jeff Bezos is an example of talent's impact on motivation and, ultimately, achievement. His plan was to study physics in college and become a leader in the field. Space exploration was his first love and physics was his profession of choice. Bezos quickly discovered that some classmates at Princeton were "wired differently" and could quickly grasp what did not come easily to him. A biographer, Brad Stone, describes the moment his limitations became clear to Bezos:

> One night during his freshman year, Bezos was struggling over a partial differential equation. After a few hours, he and his study partner visited the dorm room of a classmate, who glanced at the equation and said, "Cosine." "After we expressed some incredulousness," Bezos says, "he proceeded to draw three pages of equations that flowed through and showed that it was cosine."[20]

This experience led to what Bezos called a practical realization: There were people whose brains could process abstract concepts in physics at a level far superior to his own capabilities.[21] He knew that those who contributed to the field of theoretical physics needed to be among the top fifty in the world. They had gifts that he didn't possess. He could work harder than anyone in his field but would still not approach their level of thinking. He changed his major and earned his degree in electrical engineering and computer science. His towering talent was not in physics, despite his lifelong passion for space exploration.

Talent, however, doesn't always result in increased dedication to one's work. For some, a high level of talent can be a liability. Their talent allows them to achieve more with less effort, and they may never develop the drive and discipline needed to realize their potential. For example, the majority of child prodigies don't become luminaries in their field. A psychologist who studied these individuals noted, "When success comes too easily, prodigies are ill-prepared for what happens when the adoration goes away, their competitors start to catch up and the going gets rough."[22] Indiana University psychologist Jonathan Plucker believes that this is due in part to how others treat prodigies. "We say, 'Boy, you're really talented.' We don't say, 'Yeah, but you're still going to have to put in those 60-hour work weeks before you can make major contributions to your field.'"[23] Some lack the "rage to master" because their natural gifts allow them to be successful without a great deal of effort. They stumble when the work becomes harder and the competition better—requiring more of them than their innate talent can deliver.

Another trait of the vocationally obsessed is that they believe they are doing something that results in a larger good. The zookeepers, responding to what they saw as their duty to protect animals, fit this description. The focus is on what the individual can offer the world versus what the world can provide to the individual in the way of a career.[24] The zookeepers were not driven by self-fulfillment in the narrow sense of the term—they were responding to a larger purpose in contributing to the welfare of wild animals. Engaging in work of this type results in higher levels of motivation and a willingness to persevere when encountering setbacks. One of the best-known authorities on what motivates people at work, Barry Schwartz, concluded that most people want meaningful jobs. "You don't have to be curing cancer. . . . You can be a salesperson, or a toll collector, but if you see your goal as solving people's problems, then each day presents 100 opportunities to improve someone's life, and your satisfaction increases dramatically."[25] The desire to do meaningful work, apparent in all types of work, is even more pronounced in those who are vocationally obsessed.

There are different views on the relative importance of passion and talent in pursuing one's vocation. Some, including Steve Jobs, Elon Musk, and Jeff Bezos, suggest that the best approach is to follow one's passion, which provides the motivation needed to excel in any vocation. Their argument is that it is best to start with passion and follow where it takes you. However, others maintain that a better approach is to start by pursuing that which comes naturally, and passion will follow as time is spent working in the area in which one is uniquely gifted. A variation of this belief is the suggestion that people should focus on mastering their current occupation, even if they are not uniquely talented, and passion along with expertise will grow over time.[26] Others suggest that individuals should pursue a vocation that will benefit others. Their advice is to start by identifying a purpose greater than oneself, such as working to protect the environment. Those who believe vocation arises out of doing good suggest that it results in a deep motivation, which in turn leads to achieving more and being more satisfied than those pursuing a more self-centered goal.

Finding one's calling is often a messy process, with various combinations of passion, talent, and purpose becoming more or less important depending on the individual and his or her social environment. These three factors inevitably overlap, and for some people one approach may be more useful than the others—resulting in multiple yet equally viable paths. Each individual needs to determine his or her path with input and support from others such as mentors and family members. The following ways of thinking can help those in pursuit of their vocational calling:

- Imagine that your daily activities, at work and beyond, will occur in an endless repetition with nothing new introduced. The repeating loop is not just reliving what you enjoy— this hypothetical replay also includes experiences that are frustrating or even painful. The vocationally obsessed will answer yes when asked if this loop is something they would embrace. Others might view the repetition as a living hell—a prison from which they can't escape.[27] The philosopher Nietzsche, exploring more generally what constitutes a good life, called this "the eternal reoccurrence." He believed it was a way to determine if an individual was living the life he or she was meant to live.[28] If the prospect of reliving your current work life, both good and bad, is something you would embrace, chances are you have found your vocation.

- Those in search of vocation can also consider times when they engage in a task and lose sense of time. In these situations, the individual is entirely present in the activity with a loss of self-consciousness. The activity itself, not the potential outcome, results in a high level of engagement. It challenges the individual in a manner that matches his or her capabilities and, as a result, is highly stimulating and pleasurable. Mihaly Csikszentmihalyi, the psychologist famous for his work in this area, describes this as being in a flow state. His research suggests that people are happiest when engaging in flow activities. Flow can also be an indicator of the vocation that one should pursue.[29] A task that completely consumes an individual is one that is tapping into something meaningful and, in some cases, worthy of pursuing as a potential vocation.

- Another way to uncover calling is to imagine being eighty years old and reflecting on a life well lived. Jeff Bezos took this approach by asking himself, at different points in his career, what he would regret when he looked back on his decisions. He said this made it clear that he needed to leave his high-paying job in New York to pursue the opportunities he saw in commercializing the internet. Bezos called his way of thinking a "regret minimization framework."[30] A different version of Bezos's approach is to consider what would make you proud if you were looking back on your life at what you had achieved. However, this pride can't be the result of four or five achievements—it needs to be one thing. This is the point made by those who suggest that your contribution, if clearly understood, can be summarized in one sentence. The legacy identified does not need to be work-related and for many will involve family, friends, or community.

- Steve Jobs suggested a slightly different approach to finding one's calling. He said that he looked in the mirror every morning and asked, "If today were the last day in my life, would I want to be doing what I am doing today?"[31] If the answer was no for days in a row, Jobs knew he needed to find something closer to his true calling. As noted earlier, he believed passion was essential to people dedicating the time and effort required to do great work and persevere in the face of setbacks. His view was that a rewarding life was impossible without meaningful work and finding one's calling was the path to living that life.

THE BENEFITS OF A VOCATIONAL CALLING

In her book *The Orchid Thief*, Susan Orlean examines the psychology of obsession by profiling those who collect orchids. Her insights suggest that people who are obsessed see themselves as being engaged in something that gives their life focus. They wake up in the morning knowing who they are, what they want to do, and the activities that will move them closer to achieving their goal. It allows them to channel their energy into something that gives their life structure and meaning. She writes,

> I was starting to believe that the reason it matters to care passionately about something is that it whittles the world

down to a more manageable size. It makes the world seem
not huge and empty but full of possibility.[32]

Going further, she notes that the obsessed see adversity as a necessary element of their quest and take pride, even pleasure, in their
ability to endure and overcome obstacles. They demonstrate their
commitment to their obsession by suffering for it. She concludes that
the obsessed are willing to pay the price to go beyond the monotony
of everyday existence, "that most people in some way or another do
strive for something exceptional, something to pursue, even at their
peril, rather than abide an ordinary life."[33]

A study conducted by the recruiting firm Korn Ferry found that
many people, while perhaps not obsessive, want to be challenged. The
researchers examined why professionals leave their jobs and found a
variety of reasons, with the most common being boredom. One-third
of the respondents said they wanted to do something that would more
fully challenge them.[34] They would take the risk of moving to another
job in hopes of doing work that would better utilize their skills and
allow them to grow as professionals. This was more important than
other motivators, including the desire to make more money. For them,
being bored is worse than being underpaid. The obsessive takes this
common desire to be challenged to the extreme in pursuing a goal that
demands the most of them.

The second benefit of obsession is it can result in a level of mastery
that few people experience. An all-consuming focus enables people
who have the innate talent to go deeper and further than others in their
chosen pursuit. Imagine the experiences of Jeff Bezos, Elon Musk,
Tavis Kalanick, and Steve Jobs in building firms that transformed
entire industries. In doing so, they overcame obstacles, including their
critics, to achieve something exceptional. Investors in Silicon Valley
thought Brian Chesky lacked the skills needed to build and manage a
high-growth company. He was trained as a designer and didn't have

a business or technology background—and was told to look for a job where he could work for someone who did.[35] Jeff Bezos faced constant criticism in Amazon's first decade for creating a business that earned little or no profit. Many well-respected people in the press and financial community said that his business was unsustainable. Elon Musk was taken to task, almost weekly, for failing to deliver on his sales and production promises at Tesla, even as he was bringing electric cars into the mainstream. Travis Kalanick was told that he would never triumph over the special-interest groups that operated what he called a taxi cartel.

Independent of their fame and wealth, these leaders have experiences beyond what most people can imagine. Author David Foster Wallace, interested in the costs and benefits of being obsessive, spent time with a top professional tennis player. Wallace wanted to know why someone would dedicate his or her entire life to a singular pursuit. He profiled Michael Joyce, then a top-100 tennis player:

> The radical compression of his attention and sense of himself have allowed him to become a transcendent practitioner of an art—something few of us get to be. They've allowed him to visit and test parts of his psychic reserves most of us do not even know for sure we have (courage, playing with violent nausea, not choking, et cetera). . . . He wants this and will pay to have it—to pursue it, let it define him—and will pay up with the regretless cheer of a man for whom issues of choice became irrelevant a long time ago.[36]

Obsession also offers the opportunity to become part of a community with similar interests, goals, and lifestyle—people with the same fixations. Pursuing a vocation, particularly one involving an audacious undertaking, creates powerful bonds. Workers in many organizations spend more time with one another than they do with their family members, and in the best situations they share a passion for their work and their company. Their work becomes part of their collective history and identity. Consider the team at Elon Musk's SpaceX and the camaraderie among those who launched the first reusable rocket as well as the first private spacecraft to dock at the International Space Station. Watch videos of the SpaceX team celebrating outside the control room after the successful launch of a Falcon rocket, and it is clear that it was a shared experience that those present will never forget.[37] Or, consider Steve Jobs's description of presenting the newly developed Mac computer to an auditorium full of people at a shareholder meeting. They gave Jobs and his team a five-minute standing ovation, and Jobs recalled looking at his Mac team in the front row with everyone crying.[38] The emotional connection among people who overcome adversity and achieve the extraordinary can be profoundly meaningful—as powerful as familial relationships.

A final, more pragmatic advantage of being obsessed is that it can advance one's career. Devoting your life to a vocational calling, what Peter Drucker called a "monomaniac on a mission," increases the likelihood of success. Jeff Bezos strives to hire "missionaries" who are completely dedicated to providing customers with superior products and services. He contrasts them with "mercenaries" who work primarily to make money. That said, all things being equal, companies recognize and reward the achievements of all-in individuals. Obsession can't be manufactured for the sake of career advancement or financial gain—but when present it is nonetheless a potential benefit, at least when managed well.

VOCATIONAL REALITIES

Obsession's benefits suggest its potential value to both individuals and organizations. One commentator noted that the way we view work has shifted over time "from *jobs* to *careers* to *callings*—from necessity to status to meaning."[39] Work now competes with or replaces religion for some as a path to personal fulfillment and the betterment of society. In today's increasingly secular world, the new religion for some is vocation—worthy of extreme levels of dedication and sacrifice.[40] Jack Ma, the founder of the Chinese e-commerce firm Alibaba, recently made headlines when he supported an all-consuming approach to work—with people as dedicated as any monk or priest. In particular, he praised a practice called "996" in China. The three digits indicate that people work 9:00 a.m. to 9:00 p.m., six days a week. Ma noted that he and colleagues worked 996 while building Alibaba into one of the largest e-commerce firms in the world. He said, "I think that being able to work 996 is a huge blessing. Many companies and many people don't have the opportunity to work 996."[41]

There are, however, those who reject the idea that vocation is all-important—believing instead that work is a way to support other more meaningful areas of life, such as family and community. To them, work is not an end in itself but a means to an end. It may be enjoyable in some situations but shouldn't displace the larger, social areas of life that it supports. They go further and argue that making work the center of life is "grim and exploitative,"[42] resulting in a society where people believe they must work long and hard if they are to have a fulfilling life. Those who criticize the glorification of work suggest it is an attempt to get people to buy into their exploitation by those who profit from their efforts—including billionaires such as Elon Musk.[43] One journalist referred to an obsession with work as professional Stockholm Syndrome—where captives identify with and support their captors as a means of survival.[44]

Those opposed to a work-based society don't buy Ma's claim that working seventy-two hours a week is a blessing. Derek Thompson writes,

> What is workism? It is the belief that work is not only necessary to economic production, but also the centerpiece

of one's identity and life's purpose; and the belief that any policy to promote human welfare must *always* encourage more work.[45]

Another opponent of a work-obsessed world writes, "A culture that worships the pursuit of extreme success will likely produce some of it. But extreme success is a falsifiable god, which rejects the vast majority of its worshippers. Our jobs were never meant to shoulder the burdens of a faith, and they are buckling under the weight."[46]

We can't assume that vocation is what all people want—or should want. Does everyone desire to have his or her work be all important? Do they want to dedicate seventy hours or more a week to their job? Do they want to sacrifice time with their spouse and children due to the demands of their job? Do they want to give up their hobbies and social engagements with friends? For some, the answer to these questions is no—the price to be paid for putting work above all else is too great.

A second consideration, less obvious but equally important, is that not everyone is capable of being vocationally obsessed. Those who are extraordinarily successful claim, in their commencement speeches and books, that passion for one's work is available to all—if only the individual persists in his or her search and stays the course. This advice is typically in the form of "don't ever give up pursuing your dream." However, just as people have a wide range of cognitive, physical, and emotional capabilities, we can assume that there are differences in the ability to invest in a vocational calling. This is different than lacking the talent needed to be successful in their calling—this is lacking the temperament needed to be all-in.

In other words, people vary in their ability to care deeply about their work—even when they want to do so. They may become bored when pursuing a single goal for an extended period. They may lack the curiosity needed to delve deeply into the complexities of their craft. Or they may not have the necessary resilience to overcome the challenges that inevitably arise when pursuing an ambitious goal. There are undoubt-edly many highly competent and dedicated people, working with the best intentions, who don't have the disposition needed to be obsessed with a vocational calling. An analogy that illustrates this point is that we all know some people who have a greater capacity to love others. They have, for whatever reason, more of the emotional depth that love requires. Everyone may want to love deeply, but some are simply better equipped to do so. Differences in the ability to be vocationally obsessed apply to people at all levels of a company, although it can seem that, to be a leader, by default, is to be consumed with the work. Some leaders, however, are not obsessive at the level of Bezos and Musk. They are most likely committed, professional, and even gritty—but that is not the same as working with an all-consuming focus and relentless drive.

We want to think that everyone has a vocation that they simply need to uncover or develop. To suggest otherwise can seem elitist or unfair. Still, recognizing that people vary in both their willingness and ability to be vocationally all-in is helpful for the individuals as well as the organizations that employ them. This acknowledges the value of being honest about what we want from work as well as our ability to be consumed by it. Then we can be deliberate about the type of work we pursue, the company in which we want to work, and the sacrifices we are willing to make.

DEFINING BALANCE

The first decision is to clarify the role of work in our life, beyond the need to make enough money to survive and, in many cases, support a family. Occupational choices are, of course, constrained by one's educational background, financial status, and the availability of jobs. Not everyone has the luxury of pursuing a vocational calling. How-ever, when pursuing a vocation is an option, the question of sacrifice is always close at hand. What price are we each willing to pay to make work the center of our life and identity?[47] Those who pursue an all-consuming vocation inevitably face personal sacrifices as well as the stress of striving to achieve something exceptional.

The sacrifices that come with being vocationally obsessed range from the minor to the significant. Working at Amazon or Tesla is not a nine-to-five job—at least for those in the managerial ranks. Bezos admits, even with some pride, that Amazon is not an easy place to work. The need to work long and hard is particularly evident in newly launched companies and in the development of new products. Reflecting on the initial period of building Microsoft, Bill Gates said, "I stopped listening to music and watching TV in my 20s. It sounds extreme, but I did it because I thought they would just distract me from thinking about software." Gates's sacrifices, while difficult for most, are minor compared to what some give up for their work. An engineer who was on the development team for Apple's Macintosh computer described the benefits and costs of doing so:

> I think if you talk to a lot of people on the Mac team, they will tell you it was the hardest they've ever worked in their life. Some of them will tell you it was, you know, the happiest they've ever been in their life, but I think all of them will tell you that it is certainly one of the most intense and cherished experiences they will ever have in their life. . . . Some of those things are not sustainable for some people. I ended up changing my entire life. I lost my wife in that process. I lost my children in that process. The whole structure of my life was just changed forever by going and working on the Mac.[48]

To follow a vocational calling is to embrace sacrifice—a reality that some forget in the positive glow associated with work that has deep meaning. Many see the result of obsession and admire those who are successful in their chosen pursuit. A professional golfer, Kevin Na, was ranked among the best juniors in the United States. Players a few years younger than Na admired him and would ask what they needed to do to achieve his level of performance. He told them that they had to live like a monk—to deliberately restrict the scope of their life to focus on golf. He recalled saying to the teens who approached him about the path to success, "How much were you willing to sacrifice to be great? It meant cutting back on hobbies, not going on dates, not going out with friends on the weekend because you need that time to practice."[49]

The decision on how much to sacrifice for one's vocation is not made once but periodically as life progresses. The hours dedicated to work at an early age may not be what is desired in our forties or fifties. A single-minded fixation on work may be impossible, or at least more difficult, after we are married, have children, or are responsible for elderly parents. Even without these demands, the intensity of someone in his or her twenties and thirties can be hard to maintain with each passing decade. The photographer Annie Leibovitz noted as much when she said that she is at times envious of her younger self because the work she produced at an earlier age was so pure and energetic:

> You know, I was obsessed. Everything was about photography. I had my camera with me all the time and I lived with my camera. On some level, to grow up for me was having to wean myself from all that—to start to have a life.[50]

Part of the challenge in being honest about what we want from our work is dealing with others' expectations. Those who don't want work to consume their life may be uncomfortable saying so in industries and companies where working around the clock is valued and expected. Author Gianpiero Petriglieri notes that companies are expecting more and more from their employees—with some wanting their people to value work above all else. "The ultimate taboo in most working cultures today is to say, 'I do this just for the money, and I find great meaning in my church, in my charity, in my sports, in my family.' We equate talent with your willingness to put work at the center of your life."[51] Telling colleagues, or at least a supervisor, that you want to leave work at 5:00 p.m. each day and not work over the weekend can be difficult in a firm such as Tesla or Amazon.

On the other extreme, there are those who value work above all else. They feel most at home at work—most alive when working. But being honest about the central role of work can also be uncomfortable. Imagine telling your spouse or children that your work comes first, taking priority over family concerns and activities. Making such a confession to coworkers can also be difficult, at least in companies that emphasize the importance of work-life balance or in communities where family or religious activities are most important. Some view work-obsessed individuals as having lost perspective on what truly matters in life as a result of being addicted to their vocation.

We can assume that most people seek to avoid these two extremes and want both fulfilling work and a rich personal life. They juggle the ongoing tensions and trade-offs between their work and life outside of work. Jeff Bezos believes that "work-life-balance" is a misleading term because it suggests a trade-off between work and personal life. He prefers the term "work-life harmony," thinking that success in one realm supports success in the other.[52] A good home-life supports a good work-life, and a good work-life supports a good home-life:

> It actually is a circle. It's not a balance. If I am happy at home, I come into the office with tremendous energy. And if I am happy at work, I come home with tremendous energy. You never want to be that guy—and we all have a coworker who's that person—who, as soon as they come into a meeting, they drain all the energy out of the room. . . . You

want to come into the office and give everyone a kick in their step.[53]

Bezos's concept is more idealistic than realistic for those facing tough choices managing the conflicts that inevitably arise between work and personal life. There are trade-offs and disappointments when one area takes priority over another. Saying that harmony is the goal doesn't make it easier to achieve or any less painful. It is tough to tell your child that you can't make his or her soccer match due to work demands—or tell your teammates that you can't make an important meeting because of a family event. I can only assume that some people working at Amazon are amused when Bezos talks about harmony, as he is the architect of the company's intense and demanding work environment.

The first step, then, is to decide the desired role of work in our life. The task is then to make choices consistent with our desired level of commitment—and live with the consequences. Christine Lagarde, president of the European Central Bank, has talked of the sacrifices she made in spending less time with her family due to the demands of her vocation:

> I had to accept I could not be successful at everything, you draw up priorities and you accept a lot of guilt. . . . But that sense of guilt fades away over time. As you age, it reduces because children grow up, grandchildren arrive and you sort of reconcile yourself with what you have done.[54]

There is a cost to whatever decision we make about work and, more generally, vocation. Those who believe work is primarily a means to an end, a way to support what they deem to be the more essential aspects of life, may experience less occupational success. Simply stated, work is not as important to them as their family, community, religion, or personal life—and they thus limit the time and energy given to it. Travis

Kalanick, when questioned about the demanding pace at Uber and the impact on work-life balance, noted, "Look, if somebody's producing more, they're going to rise faster. That just is. There's no way around that."[55] For those who are vocationally obsessed, there is also a price to pay, often in terms of their health and relationships. They may also sacrifice a great deal in the pursuit of their vocation and not achieve success—and may ultimately question later in life if they made the right choice in putting work above all else. For those in the middle, they must manage the ongoing trade-offs and tensions in striving to meet both work and personal demands.

FINDING THE RIGHT ENVIRONMENT

After determining the role of vocation in one's life, the goal is to find a company that supports that decision. The choice of where to work is critically important. Take the person who decides to pursue a vocational calling. In the best situations, the interests of a company and its members align—with each benefiting from their shared obsession. Companies vary in the degree to which they expect their members to be all-in. Obsessive behavior that is considered inappropriate at one company may be valued in another company.

Consider the engineer who worked for a firm that expected him to always respond to emails from his colleagues, and particularly his supervisors, within a few hours including weekends. He took a job at another firm that reprimanded him for sending emails out late at night and over the weekend to his colleagues. His new firm didn't want people working all hours of the day and all days of the week, and he was violating a norm they had established to promote better work-life balance. Depending on one's view of work, this could be a positive norm or one that is highly frustrating. Because of these organizational differences, some companies are a better fit for the obsessed in terms of their culture and work practices. In a related sense, the obsessed also need supervisors and colleagues who are like themselves in their views about their work and the ideal work culture. Being surrounded by like-minded people with similar traits and capabilities is highly motivating to them. Inversely, working with less dedicated people can be demotivating for those who are all-in.

A study conducted in the United States Air Force Academy suggests the frustration that highly motivated colleagues are likely to experience when they work in a team with others who are less committed. The researchers studied the physical fitness of almost thirty-five hundred cadets during their four years of study.[56] They wanted to understand why some individuals improved more than others in their physical conditioning. They found that the level of fitness varied significantly by squadron, each composed of about thirty cadets who lived and worked together. There was a correlation between a cadet's improvement in physical fitness and how fit he or she was on entering the Academy, which was not a surprise. Those who were fitter were more likely to improve.

However, almost as important was the level of fitness across each squadron and, in particular, the fitness of the least fit cadet in each squadron. Most would assume that the fittest person in a group, or the person with the greatest leadership capabilities, would be the most important in determining the group's overall fitness (by motivating others to higher levels of performance). Surprisingly, the findings indicate that a less-disciplined cadet eroded the performance of the entire group. The impact of the least fit was most pronounced on those who also trended toward less physical fitness—in essence, the *less fit* followed the *least fit*. If we extrapolate from physical fitness to other work-related situations, the implication for those who are all-in is that they may have less influence on peers than those who are less motivated. In other words, behavior in groups has a contagious element that is not always what we would expect. A takeaway from this research is to choose your peers carefully.[57]

The choice of environment is also important for the most accomplished individuals. As noted earlier, a total commitment to work will likely result in a higher level of performance. That being so, consider the results of the research team that studied 414 hairstylists working in 120 salons in Taiwan. Based on their findings, they concluded that high performers are both supported and undermined by their colleagues.[58] High performers are supported by their peers who believe they can potentially benefit by working with them, by improving the performance of the group, by helping them develop their capabilities, and by obtaining greater resources for the group as a result of their contributions. The researchers describe this as high performers offering greater "resource access" to the others in their group.

Team members, however, can also undermine high performers. The concern is that the high performers make those performing at a lower level appear less capable and less dedicated to their work. They can also evoke envy because they can attract more attention, are given better career opportunities, or have access to greater resources than their less successful colleagues. The result is that lower-performing team members will question how they can keep pace with someone who is more talented and motivated. High performers also can be undermined by those who are equally talented, who see them as a competitive threat to their sense of self-worth and career advancement. This undermining of high performers in a group can be overt or subtle. In some cases, they are negatively labeled ("he is not very strategic"), have rumors spread about them ("she takes credit for the work of others"), are blamed when things go wrong ("he didn't give us what we need to deliver on our plan"), or are isolated from social interactions ("let's not invite her to our social gathering"). The researchers speculated that the combination of being both supported and undermined can confuse and raise the anxiety of high performers (even more than only being undermined).[59] The obsessed thus need to be deliberate in selecting a work environment that meets their needs, focusing in partciular on the talent and commitment of one's potential peers.

A final consideration in selecting a place to work is the degree to which an organization will take advantage of commitment. The companies profiled in this book, firms such as Amazon, Tesla, and Uber, have a history of pushing their people very hard. They can do so, in part, because of the dedication of their members to the company's purpose and the work itself. In some situations, the obsessed will willingly go along with excessive demands because they are doing what matters most to them. They are being used because they want to be of use. The downside is that they can care too much and accept, or even embrace, extreme work demands.[60] Elon Musk and Jeff Bezos have indicated that the culture of their firms is a good fit for some but not others. Individuals need to be realistic about the work challenges they will face and, perhaps even more importantly, the culture of the company they are joining relative to the role of work in their life.

DEVELOPING PRODUCTIVE ROUTINES

One key to success is to recognize when obsession has become counterproductive or even toxic. This is an ongoing challenge because obsession doesn't naturally foster self-awareness or self-regulation. Thus the obsessed are always at risk of self-destructive behavior. Alex Ohanian, the founder of Reddit, believes this is even more likely in industries such as technology, where it is more common for people to glorify their excessive work practices. In doing so, they use social media to note their long hours and around-the-clock dedication to work. Ohanian uses the term "hustle porn" to describe the exaltation of all-encompassing work. He says,

> This is one of the most toxic, dangerous things in tech
> right now. This idea that unless you are suffering, grinding,

working every hour of every day, you're not working hard enough.[61]

Ohanian and others argue that it is essential to establish healthy physical and emotional routines that reduce the likelihood of obsession with work becoming a significant risk. Steve Magness, a coach to long-distance runners, believes that the key to performing at a high level over time is the ability to focus intensely and push hard to excel in a targeted area and then take time to rest and recover. He describes this as "stress + rest = growth."[62] He believes that stress in the pursuit of a challenging goal can be both productive and destructive—depending on how the individual manages it. The key is to push hard to excel, but no more than the mind and body can take without becoming completely exhausted. He argues that getting outside of one's comfort zone promotes learning and ultimately better performance. Equally important, however, is taking time to disconnect from the challenging activity and adapt from the stress it places on the individual. He shows how the best athletes in the world develop approaches that produce the right amount of stress and rest—with both being necessary to perform at a high level.

Academic research supports the benefit of being able to disengage from one's fixation periodically. Professor Robert Vallerand has conducted numerous studies on the psychology of passion.[63] He believes passion comes in two forms: harmonious and obsessive. Harmonious passion is evident when people are doing something that they love but don't allow it to overwhelm other aspects of their life. They can decide when to engage in the activity, as well as when they want to focus on other activities. Those with an obsessive passion, in contrast, don't have control over their passions; that is, they can't stop engaging in the passionate activity even when it conflicts and potentially harms other areas of their life. They are constantly thinking about work even when engaged in other activities. Vallerand developed a survey to identify those who are obsessively passionate and found that they are more likely to say that the following statements describe how they feel:[64]

- I have difficulties controlling my urge to do my work.
- My work is the only thing that really turns me on.
- If I could, I would only do my work.
- I have the impression that my work controls me.

Vallerand concludes that obsessive passion, where the individual can't detach from his or her work, is detrimental to one's physical, mental, and social well-being.

Consider what rest looks like for Jeff Bezos. He has said that he makes sure to get eight hours of sleep or more each night. He leisurely starts his day, typically reading the paper and spending time with family. He arranges his work schedule so the most demanding tasks are in the late morning when he finds himself at his cognitive peak. He typically doesn't work late and finds time for rigorous exercise regularly. He also takes regular vacations with family and friends to a range of far-flung locations.[65] Contrast his approach to Elon Musk who didn't take a vacation for years and by most accounts regularly works one hundred hours a week. Musk has said that his schedule is primarily the result of the challenges facing Tesla, but he also recognizes his inability to disengage from his work. While respecting Musk's commitment to achieving the extraordinary, most would assume that Bezos has a personal and professional routine that is more sustainable over time and perhaps even more productive. Arianna Huffington, one of the founders of *Huffington Post* and a former Uber board member, wrote an open letter to Musk suggesting that his approach will fail:

> Working 120-hour weeks doesn't leverage your unique qualities, it wastes them. You can't simply power through—that's just not how our bodies and our brains work. Nobody knows

better than you that we can't get to Mars by ignoring the laws of physics. Nor can we get where we want to go by ignoring scientific laws in our daily lives.[66]

Each person needs to determine a routine that serves him or her best in recovering from the demands of work. For some, this might be committing to not working past a specific hour of the day, taking time on the weekends to completely shut off from work and colleagues, or scheduling periodic vacations to provide the time needed to relax and recharge.

Another approach that some use to avoid potential burnout is to eliminate professional and personal distractions that consume time and energy. Psychological research suggests that people only have so much cognitive bandwidth and that each decision consumes some of what is available. Even the most intelligent individuals will wear down if they are making too many decisions on a given day. Recognizing their limits, some eliminate activities that consume their time and, more importantly, their decision-making reserves. They may settle on a regular diet that they follow each day. They may simplify their dress to alleviate the need to decide what to wear each morning. Instead, they settle on a personal "uniform" that requires no choice on their part. More significant alternations can complement these relatively minor changes, in areas such as how much and with whom they socialize or their level of involvement in outside activities or hobbies. The goal is to remove distractions and eliminate decisions that take time and energy away from one's vocation.

A third routine that is helpful is to seek periodic feedback on managing one's vocational choice—both professionally and personally. Obtaining helpful feedback requires discipline in periodically asking for input from others. It also requires building relationships with a few trusted sources of input and support—be they family members, team colleagues, or external advisors. These are confidants who can listen to concerns and offer useful—and sometimes tough—feedback. Everyone has blind spots, and obsessives are more vulnerable than most.[67] Steve Jobs believed that a great team is one where each member counterbalances the weaknesses of others, working in a manner that keeps their negative qualities in check. Feedback can also come from outsiders if those individuals have sufficient exposure to provide useful advice. Those providing feedback need to have a deep understanding of the obsessive individual's strengths and weaknesses, as well as the work challenges he or she is facing. They can be particularly helpful when an obsession has gone too far—causing potential harm to the individual and the goal he or she is pursuing. The person can help the obsessive take a step back, consider his or her actions, and make changes as needed to avoid the pitfalls of being all-in.

The challenge is that obsessives can be confident to the point of being arrogant, especially when they are successful. As a result, they may not want feedback and, when it does occur, can discount or ignore the advice. As noted earlier, reports suggest that several board members and investors attempted to influence Travis Kalanick but with limited success, at least judging by the myriad of mistakes made during his tenure. The leader needs to be self-aware enough to solicit and then listen to contrary voices on the critical issues facing the leader and his or her firm. For those striving to achieve the extraordinary, they often hear that what they want to accomplish is unlikely if not impossible. Each leader learns to trust his or her judgment, capabilities, and resourcefulness in achieving difficult things, regardless of what others think. The problem is, this mentality can also mean that leaders stop listening to valuable feedback. The risk is for the leader to become an ideologue whose beliefs are unchanging and closed to new information and points of view. Not all advice is on target, of course, but the input of others needs to be considered as a leader makes decisions. Those giving feedback, in turn, must have the credibility and skill needed to influence a hard-charging leader when he or she is at risk of self-destructing.

TAKEAWAYS

- Vocation is the belief in one's calling to engage in a specific type of work.
- The challenge is to determine the centrality of work in life and, if appropriate, the vocational path to follow.
- For those who find and embrace their vocation, the goal is to select an organization that is the best fit. The mission, culture, and practices of a firm are all important, as well as having colleagues who are equally talented and committed.
- Being vocationally obsessed is a risky undertaking. To be managed effectively, it requires physical, mental, and social routines to avoid the pitfalls of being all-in.

7

THE ORGANIZATION'S CHALLENGE:
NOURISHING OBSESSION

MANAGE YOUR OBSESSIVES OR MANAGE YOUR DECLINE

As a young woman, my mother lived in London during the German air raids of World War II. Years later, she didn't talk about her experience other than saying she hated going into the crowded city subways, which served as bomb shelters for the public. She preferred taking her chances aboveground. The German air campaign sent waves of bombers over the country, mostly at night. The goal was to destroy Britain's industrial and maritime capabilities, break the morale of its citizens, and allow for an eventual invasion of the country. The Blitz ended after eight months once Germany realized it would not produce the intended results and redirected its air force to the invasion of Russia. Three years later, Germany once again attacked London but with a radical new weapon—the V2, the world's first long-range ballistic missile.

The "vengeance weapon"[1] was the creation of Werner von Braun. From the time he was a boy, his passion was space exploration. He believed he would build a rocket that would allow humans to go to the moon and eventually Mars. He wrote of his desire to be a member of the first expedition into space.

Interplanetary travel! Here was a task worth dedicating one's life to. Not just stare through a telescope at the Moon and the planets but to soar through the heavens and actually explore the mysterious universe. I knew how Columbus had felt.[2]

His brilliance as a university student was recognized by professors and government officials, resulting in von Braun being named the top civilian specialist for Germany's rocket development at age twenty. He knew that his dream of interplanetary travel would require massive sums of money, which the German military was in the best position to provide. In turn, the military wanted von Braun to develop advanced weapons, from missiles to fighter jets, that would help Germany win the war that Hitler would soon wage. Von Braun and the military believed their arrangement would be mutually beneficial—each using the other to get what they wanted.

When Nazi Germany collapsed in 1945, von Braun and members of his team surrendered to the US military. The German rocket experts were secretly relocated to the United States, first to El Paso and eventually Alabama. The US government didn't want von Braun to fall into the hands of the Russians, an ally that would soon become an adversary. The military believed von Braun and his team of scientists and engineers, the most advanced in the world at the time, would accelerate the building of ballistic weapons and space capabilities.

Von Braun, who eventually became an American citizen, held a variety of increasingly senior leadership positions in the US Army and then the space agency NASA. He was a crucial figure in the US efforts to develop the world's leading space program, providing technical and organizational leadership that was invaluable. He also appeared in popular magazines, TV shows, and educational films with celebrities such as Walt Disney, gaining public and government support for the exploration of space. His contributions in developing the Saturn V rocket were essential in landing the first person on the moon, with some suggesting that the US could not have done so without his leadership.[3] A historian at NASA believes that von Braun was the most influential rocket engineer and space advocate of his time—a complex and controversial figure who played the most significant role in "selling the idea of spaceflight and making it come true."[4]

The extent to which von Braun would go to advance his dreams of space became more apparent over time. Historical records indicated that he joined the Nazi party and later became an SS officer.[5] After the war he said he had little choice given the pressure placed on him by senior Nazi military and political figures. He also said he regretted the civilian deaths caused by his rockets but emphasized that there were victims on both sides of the war, and that "a war is a war, and when my country is at war, my duty is to help win that war."[6] The most benign view of von Braun's war history is that he was a patriotic German, doing what was needed to support his country while advancing his work on space exploration.

People began to question von Braun's portrayal of himself as a "good German" once it became widely known that slave laborers, mostly Russian and Jewish concentration camp prisoners, were forced to work in appalling conditions to assemble his rockets. When pressed, he claimed he was ignorant of the use of forced labor and the deaths of thousands who worked in the production facilities. He claimed that he was working in a research complex hundreds of miles from the primary assembly plants and was not responsible for what occurred there. Some historical records and witnesses, however, suggest that von Braun visited the plants at least a dozen times and observed, if not approved, the inhumane conditions and brutality toward prisoners.[7] In his later years, he privately expressed remorse for the use of slave labor but stated that he did not participate in the abuse or have the power to stop it.

Governments, as well as organizations and teams, will sometimes go to great lengths to benefit from what talented obsessives have to offer.[8]

The US government viewed von Braun as one of the most prominent scientists in Germany—one they wanted on the US side in an anticipated arms race with Russia. Others believe that von Braun should have been tried for war crimes, as were other high-ranking German officials such as Albert Speer. However, in 1945, the US government did not prosecute him—instead, senior political and military officials valued what he could bring to the development of new weapons in an era of emerging Cold War tensions. They wanted to benefit from his pioneering technical work on the V2, as well as what one colleague called an "uncanny organizing ability."[9] Once in the US, the actions of von Braun during the war were downplayed or ignored by the government, replaced with a public relations campaign that made him a hero to many Americans at the start of the space age. His complicated place in history is suggested by that fact the he is one of the few people ever photographed with Adolf Hitler and, decades later, President John F. Kennedy.

Von Braun's relevance is in how his life illustrates obsession's contradictory nature. His life story is one where "the good and the bad are all mixed up."[10] His singularity of purpose and unyielding drive resulted in remarkable achievements. Von Braun was the force behind the first rocket to reach the edge of outer space in 1942, the first American satellite to launch in 1958, and the rockets that sent astronauts to the moon in 1969. His obsession also resulted in him tolerating, if not supporting, the horrors of the Nazi era.[11] By some accounts, von Braun was apolitical and only concerned with how to best advance his dreams of space exploration. Von Braun's legacy is still under debate, with his supporters viewing him as a technological visionary caught in historical forces that he couldn't control. His detractors see him as an immoral opportunist who enthusiastically worked for a barbaric Nazi regime and, at the very least, was a bystander to abuse and suffering. An editorial at the time of von Braun's death described him as "a man so possessed of a vision, an intellectual hunger, that any accommodation may be justified in its pursuit."[12] What is not in debate is his all-consuming obsession with advancing space exploration, which he believed would benefit humankind.[13]

Using von Braun as an example of obsession's potential is not to suggest that what goes on in corporate offices is at all equivalent to the atrocities of the Nazi regime. Von Braun's life in its extremes, however, does illustrate how obsession can be a force for good and bad, and how it needs to be carefully managed by individuals and organizations. Two questions are particularly important in examining obsession's impact:

- For the individual: How far am I willing to go to pursue my obsession? Where do I draw the line in my drive to achieve my goal?
- For the organization: How far are we willing to go to support an obsessive individual who can contribute to our success? Where do we draw the line in what we will tolerate?

It may seem obvious that organizations want obsessives, as they will benefit from the obsessive's total dedication to achieving something exceptional. What company doesn't strive to hire and retain those who give their all to the realization of an ambitious goal? However, embracing obsessives is more complicated. Consider the actions of Elon Musk, which resulted in Musk and Tesla being sued for fraud by the Securities and Exchange Commission (SEC). The initial complaint came after Musk posted statements on Twitter indicating that he had "funding secured" for the potential privatization of his company. Tesla's stock rose on his tweet and the SEC took notice. Its legal action resulted in a settlement that included a significant fine for Musk and Tesla ($20 million each), Musk stepping down as chairman of Tesla, and an agreement to have his future communications—at least as they potentially impact the firm's stock—internally vetted before being distributed.[14]

Musk defended his tweet and was highly critical of the SEC, but he later admitted that he was prone to mistakes because of his excessive work hours and the stress of solving Tesla's production problems. A broader interpretation of Musk's communication is that it arose from his hatred of short sellers, whom he believes were undermining him and the company he loved. Some speculate that his tweet was an attempt to drive up Tesla's stock price and punish the short sellers, who would lose money if that occurred.[15] Obsessive leaders love their products and companies to a degree beyond what most people can comprehend—it is akin to the love a parent feels for his or her child. Musk's complete commitment to Tesla results in him striving to protect it from those he views as critics—even if he unintentionally causes more harm than good in doing so.

Corporations and their shareholders want growth but also value predictability and control. Reason and logic, however, can suffer in the pursuit of an obsession. No wonder that some firms, and their shareholders, come to believe that obsessive leaders require more attention, money, and risk than they are worth. Steve Jobs left Apple in 1994 because his firm's board would not back him and his plans. They also believed he was creating unproductive conflicts, favoring his own projects over what they believed was best for the company. Travis Kalanick was pushed to resign his CEO role because shareholders concluded his decisions and behavior had irrevocably undermined his leadership credibility and was damaging the Uber brand.

The best companies know they need to attract, manage, and support productively obsessive leaders—even when these individuals can be difficult personalities and prone to making mistakes. They are typically not "company" men and women, as the work is more important to them than the rules and procedures established by senior leadership. Steve Jobs described Apple as an Ellis Island company built by those whom he described as refugees from other companies that failed to give them the autonomy and support they desired.

DETERMINE THE ORGANIZATION'S OBSESSIVE FOCUS

The first step in managing obsession is for the organization to be clear on what matters most—in other words, to be clear on its obsession. The most central obsession, one common to the leaders profiled in this book, is the unrelenting drive to improve that which currently exists. Jeff Bezos, Elon Musk, and Travis Kalanick all worked to replace "what is" with something better—either a product or service superior to that offered by competitors or even that currently provided by their firms. The obsessive leader who is innovative is at war with the status quo, believing that creating something better is a competitive and societal necessity. Amazon, for instance, has methodically reduced shipping times—and in so doing improved both service to its customers and the performance of its competitors (who must keep pace by improving their capabilities).

Having a cadre of all-in individuals, focused in the right way, is particularly crucial at certain points in a firm's history. This may be during a start-up phase when a company is striving to displace more established competitors, as Amazon did when it went up against a much larger Barnes & Noble, as well as Tesla in competing with major car manufacturers such as VW and GM. Obsession is also needed when an established firm is under assault by a new competitor. Consider the challenges facing Walmart and Target, whose leaders must determine how their firms will compete in a rapidly changing retail industry. A 9-to-5 mentality, particularly in the leadership ranks, will not suffice when competing against a firm with the ambition and capabilities of Amazon. Those who lack what obsession provides will sooner or later fall behind their competition and eventually fail. This is even more likely in highly competitive and volatile industries where the rules of competition are being rewritten. For example, the Ford Motor Company is attempting to compete with the likes of Google and Tesla to develop autonomous vehicles. To do so, Ford and its partners will spend billions over the new few years. Ford will need to build a team of people with the talent and commitment required to create a better product than their world-class competitors. It also needs a company culture that supports these individuals and doesn't bog them down with beliefs and practices that inhibit innovation and risk-taking. Ford may face significant challenges in attracting and retaining the people it needs—in part because its corporate culture was formed over decades of operating in a slow-moving, lower-tech environment.

As noted in chapter 3, Jeff Bezos believes that there are many options regarding potential areas of obsessive focus, and each firm needs to determine what works best in its industry and its culture. The growth of the firms outlined in this book suggests that fixating on customers or products is most likely to result in an enduring company. Contrast this with firms that fixate on near-term financial results or on beating their competition. Once the focus is clear, the task is making it more than a slogan. Many firms claim that customers are their primary focus. However, to build a customer-first culture along with robust practices to serve them is a difficult task. Saying that you are customer obsessed is easy, but being obsessed is hard.

Another common mistake is to embrace a range of potential obsessions and not prioritize what is most important. The result is striving to be all things to all people, and lacking the clarity and discipline to have a dominant guiding principle of utmost importance. Being exceptional in one area is exceedingly difficult, and trying to be exceptional in three or four areas can be counterproductive (by confusing people on what is truly the top priority, and by allocating resources in a manner that makes superior execution less likely). Focusing on a top priority doesn't mean that a leader or company ignores other areas. In the best cases, other beliefs and practices exist to support the firm's dominant obsession. Amazon wants its products, such as the Kindle and Echo, to be superb devices and strives to make them better with each iteration. But customer obsession is clearly the guiding force in everything it does.

SELECT YOUR STRUCTURAL MODEL

The next task is to determine what organizational model is needed to achieve a firm's obsession. One approach is to create a special forces group with a company—a cadre of carefully selected individuals who work to solve a difficult challenge for the benefit of the organization. This group is comprised of a select few, resulting in a smaller cadre of talented and dedicated individuals within a company. This use of the term "special forces" in this case means that not everyone needs to reach an obsessive level of commitment.

One justification for a special forces approach is that not everyone has the ability or desire to be all-in. As noted in the last chapter, people reside at different points along a continuum, one that ranges from apathy to interest, passion, and finally obsession. The ideal, in some cases, is for an organization to create a smaller group of obsessives while having a general employee population that is engaged and professional but not consumed with their work. This model is similar to the US military, where elite groups such as the Navy SEALs are carefully selected and trained to operate at a level beyond other service men and women. The attrition rate for those seeking to become SEALs is high because of the extreme physical and mental demands placed on them. Those who make it through the training are the elite—individuals who have the physical, mental, and emotional capabilities needed to take on the most demanding tasks.

In corporate life, those in such roles typically work in special project teams. For example, they might be responsible for designing and bringing to market an innovative technology that is needed for a company to grow. The Apple Mac team, mentioned earlier, is an example of a special forces group.

A more aggressive organizational model is to go beyond a small number of talented and driven individuals and strive to build an entire company obsessed with its mission. Elon Musk uses the term "special forces" to refer to his entire organization and the need for everyone to be a top performer. Developing and sustaining obsession at an organizational level is clearly much harder given the variance in people's willingness to invest in their work. It works against the tendency of most organizations to become more complacent and bureaucratic once they achieve a level of success. Successful firms have the luxury of being less intense and driven. An "all hands" model is harder to achieve because of the difficulty of fostering a high level of focus and commitment across an entire workforce. That said, this is the goal of firms such as Amazon, Tesla, and Uber.

These two models, special forces and all-hands, are not mutually exclusive. A hybrid approach may be the ideal. This would involve a general population that commits as much as possible to the firm's obsession, with a threshold necessary for each colleague. Within that larger group, there can also be a smaller cadre that is willing and able to give much more.

These two models result in different challenges in attracting, motivating, and retaining productively obsessive individuals. For instance, a special forces model can result in a status hierarchy within a company (since those in the elite groups receive more attention, resources, and recognition). If not carefully managed, this can result in an "us versus them" divide. This occurred at Apple when Steve Jobs's Mac team, one that he described as a group of pirates, which at times operated in a manner that caused opposition to "Apple's navy", alienated colleagues and caused schisms across the company.[16] This team also produced the Mac computer, which introduced revolutionary features that changed the role of computers in our lives. The Mac team demonstrated in the extreme both the strengths and weaknesses of a special forces model.

Companies today are increasingly focused on valuing and supporting diversity across a variety of dimensions. An area that is not typically discussed in terms of diversity is the role of work in people's lives. In the extreme, some see their work as a means to an end and others view it as an end in itself. These are not binary positions since people often want a combination of both. However, there are real differences in attitudes about work, and companies need to determine how they will value and support people at different places along the obsession continuum. There are significant differences in how people view the role of work in their lives—and companies can't assume that everyone has the same perspective or needs.

One approach is to push for work being all-important, even when a company may emphasize the importance of work-life balance. The companies profiled in this book all have intense work environments that demand much of their people. The other approach is to create a less intense environment that respects the need for a life outside of work. These two approaches are not mutually exclusive, but companies need to select one or the other—and then manage the downsides of the approach selected.

HIRE A CRITICAL MASS OF OBSESSIVES

The third task is to attract and retain a sufficient number of people with the mind-set and capabilities needed to advance a firm's obsession. The number will vary depending on the structural model selected (the special forces and all-hands approaches have different talent requirements). In either case, obsessive individuals seek out organizations that allow them to work on what matters most to them. Those who work at Tesla or SpaceX know that they are building some of the most innovative products in the world. They are also attracted to the impact that these products will have on society. A company should not be designed to appeal to all people—instead, it should have a clear focus that attracts those who share a similar passion for the company's mission and who are a good fit with its culture. Once the firm's obsession is well articulated, those who share it will be attracted to it and, all things being equal, more likely to remain.

Each company still needs to design a process that screens for those who are the best fit with its particular focus and culture. Amazon and

Tesla want their hires to have specific capabilities, such as the ability to solve complex problems. Musk will probe the role an engineering applicant had in the development of a product, asking for specific details about his or her contribution and how problems were solved. More generally, Tesla wants people who are obsessed with product excellence while Amazon looks for a customer focus in its hires. The goal is to identify those who are passionate about what matters most to the firm.

Interview questions about the ability to be productively obsessive include:

- Give an example of when you overcame adversity to achieve something extraordinary. What specifically did you do to deliver the result? [Look for details that indicate a deep level of involvement.]
- Describe an ideal day at work for you. What are you doing/producing?
- Imagine that we offer you a position that fits your interests but offers less visibility and impact than an equivalent position in another part of the company. Which position would you prefer and why?
- Describe a time when you were lost in your work—when you were highly engaged in the task itself.
- Tell me about a time when you pursued a goal, in your personal or professional life, to an unreasonable degree.

Interview questions about fit with the firm's obsession:

- Why do you want to join our firm/group? [Probe for fit with firm's obsession.]
- What do you look for in those with whom you want to work as colleagues and team members? [Probe for fit with firm's obsession.]

- Imagine you have worked with us for ten years. Looking back, what would give you the most pride in what you achieved? [Probe for fit with firm's obsession.]
- Tell me about an experience that illustrates your commitment to [insert firm's obsession such as delighting customers, creating superior products. . . .].
- Tell me about a time you had to deal with a difficult challenge, for example, customer concerns, product design flaws, and so forth. What did you do to resolve it?
- How do you plan to ensure that your focus is always on improving [insert relevant issue, such as customer experience, product performance, and so forth]?
- To what extent do you enjoy beating a competitor [versus delighting customers, designing innovative products, etc.]?

The other imperative, beyond attracting the right people, is sustaining a culture that is focused and driven. As discussed earlier, this is why Bezos stresses the need for what he calls a Day 1 mentality. This involves a number of cultural reinforcing practices, including approaches that ensure that each person is contributing to what the company needs to be successful. Most start-ups operating in a Day 1 mode can't afford to carry people who lack the skill and drive needed for their company to grow. One of the hardest decisions a leader makes is removing those who have significantly contributed to a firm's success but who don't have what is needed to do so in the future. Steve Jobs, similar to Bezos and Musk, believed that great products and services don't happen without the best talent. Most leaders voice that point of view, but fewer leaders act on those who fail to meet their expectations. Steve Jobs said that he was responsible for ensuring that the top one hundred people at Apple were "A-players." Early in his career, Jobs concluded that the contributions of the best software and hardware engineers was one hundred times that of those whom he called B- and C-players. He thus worked hard to find and keep A-players, those he believed were essential to building great products. He also said the Mac Team taught him that A-players want to work with other A-players—and it was his job, and the job of his leadership team, to remove less talented people from the company. He wanted to prevent what he condescendingly called a "bozo explosion," which occurs when those who are not A-players remain with the company.[17]

PROVIDE MEANINGFUL ASSIGNMENTS

Having attracted people with the necessary talent and traits, an organization must then engage them appropriately. Obsessives care most about doing work that matters. It is particularly essential to provide obsessives with impactful projects that match their interests. The other managerial imperative is to not burden them with administrative tasks that take them away from their work. Policies, procedures, and processes inevitably expand as a firm grows, often out of necessity to manage its increased size and complexity. However, this can result in a burdensome bureaucracy that is especially objectionable to those with an obsessive personality—who hate being distracted by what they view as non-valued added activities. An example noted earlier was when Levandowski, the head of the autonomous vehicle group at Google, bought a hundred cars to use in his testing of the technology. He didn't want the delay of going through the company's formal authorization process, so he billed the cost of the cars back to the company on his expense report. He may have also wanted to send a message to senior leadership about the bureaucracy that he believed was getting in the way of acting fast to seize new opportunities in a rapidly evolving industry.

The challenge for growing companies is to sustain an environment that is attractive to obsessives. One way that Amazon does so is by creating small teams with challenging objectives. Bezos is well known for saying that teams at Amazon are expected to be small enough to feed their members with only two pizzas.[18] Using small teams allows for each person to see the impact of contributions, which increases individual and team accountability for results. The culture of Amazon minimizes the "free-loader effect," which is more likely to occur in larger teams where less dedicated or less talented members can benefit from the hard work of others. Small teams also reduce the time required to effectively communicate and coordinate efforts, which often consumes valuable time in larger groups.

During the leadership tenure of Steve Jobs, Apple also gave obsessives what they wanted by doing away with committees and having a single point of leadership for each functional area.[19] Each had total accountability for delivering what Jobs expected. He believed in hiring superior talent and giving them clear responsibility for delivering results. His VPs knew that he practiced "no excuse" management, where people at the senior levels were expected to deliver regardless of the challenges they faced. They were all working in service of the Apple platform and rewarded based on the company's overall performance. In his mind this was more effective than falling back on rigorous processes or spreading ownership among the members of cross-functional teams. He said he designed Apple to be a huge start-up company with himself at the center—with small focused teams, each led by a talented and accountable leader, reporting to him.[20]

ESTABLISH WELL-DESIGNED CHECKS AND BALANCES

The above approaches increase the likelihood of attracting and retaining obsessives. It is a mistake, however, to give these individuals complete latitude in how they operate as they may behave irresponsibly in the pursuit of their goals. In some firms, obsessives face few consequences for their actions because they achieve results. Uber allowed Travis Kalanick too much leeway in his aggressive approach to growing the firm. Arianna Huffington, then on Uber's board, said that there would be no tolerance for those who act improperly. "One of the things I said in my first all-hands [meeting] when I spoke to the employees was that going forward, we would end the cult of the top performer. . . . When you deliver results, somehow a lot is forgiven. And that is particularly prevalent in the Valley. So, I called the top performers brilliant jerks and I said, 'We're going to have zero tolerance for them.'"[21]

Companies with obsessive leaders need formal and informal processes to prevent destructive acts. Of primary importance is clarifying what is considered out-of-bounds behavior for leaders and their teams. At Uber, Kalanick's growth mentality permeated the company's culture and resulted in actions that eroded the goodwill of a significant number of its customers, drivers, and employees. Advisors and colleagues can play a pivotal role in preventing such outcomes if they are able to intervene when an obsessive leader acts in irresponsible ways. As noted in chapter 5, Garrett Camp was in a position to have a positive influence on Travis Kalanick. We don't know what he did to temper Kalanick's misdeeds, but we do know that Kalanick continued to act in ways that damaged Uber.

It is not easy to challenge or place limits on a forceful leader such as Kalanick, one who is largely responsible for creating one of the fastest-growing firms in history. This is particularly the case for members of a leader's team, as confronting one's boss with tough feedback and advice can be difficult if not career-limiting in some companies. Failing to do so, however, can result in a leader's downfall and harm to his or her firm. In the case of Uber, someone such as Camp should have worked harder or more skillfully to prevent Kalanick from self-destructing.

In a related manner, an obsessive leader can benefit from colleagues who can act in a manner that lessens the leader's downsides.

A programmer who worked at Apple said that Henri Lamiraux, then vice president of software engineering, played a constructive role in softening the destructive side of Steve Jobs's management style. He described Lamiraux as a "source of coolness that prevented us from constantly getting burned by Steve's searing heat."[22] In this respect a colleague can maximize what an obsessive has to offer but also minimize the various pitfalls detailed in this book. This is a difficult role to play because the colleague needs the trust and support of both the obsessive leader and those at lower levels of the organization. This individual can't become an apologist for bad behavior on the part of the leader. In the best case, he or she can work in a manner that produces a better outcome for the leader, his or her team, and the organization.

Another safeguard is for a governing body, such as a board, to assess a leader and the culture created within an organization. This can be an informal set of conversations with colleagues regarding a leader's behavior and how it feels working for him or her. Some leaders will resist such an assessment, viewing it as an intrusion into how they are managing their people. The goal, however, is not to find fault but to ensure that problems or issues are recognized early and addressed. A more formal approach can take the form of a periodic internal organization survey or hiring an outside consultancy or legal firm to asses a firm's internal practices. This is the typical procedure after major problems surface within a company, as was the case for Uber, but by then the damage is done. A more effective approach is to periodically conduct an assessment that surfaces problems before they became a crisis.

While safeguards are essential, a company needs to resist creating an excessive number of policies and procedures that undermine the motivation of obsessive individuals and teams. A well-designed set of safeguards provides necessary guidelines but doesn't result in people believing they are being micromanaged. The most driven and creative individuals often want a great deal of autonomy. But they are not unique—most people want more control over their work. Those who have autonomy are more satisfied with their jobs and more motivated to do great work. They are also healthier than colleagues who have little choice in how they perform their jobs.[23] The goal is for firms to attract and retain productive obsessives by creating a culture that supports them even when they are at odds with the bureaucratic mind-set and controls often found in large companies. The art is creating organizational controls that work in preventing misdeeds but don't undermine what obsessives can provide.

MANAGING OBSESSION'S PITFALLS

Even when taking the above actions, organizations need to remain vigilant regarding obsession's dark potential. Chapter 2 outlined the general dangers of obsession. There are, however, more specific challenges facing organizations that embrace an obsessive focus. The first risk is obsessing on a current business model, while neglecting larger market and social trends. Recall that obsession is the singular focus and relentless drive needed to achieve an ambitious goal. The taxi industry may have leaders who are obsessive about protecting the current transportation model from which they benefit, even in the face of better alternatives (such as Uber). We can understand why they would do that given their vested interest in maintaining the status quo. Other groups make the same mistake when they resist or ignore changes that will disrupt their industry. BlackBerry, maker of what was once the most popular smartphone, didn't think the iPhone would threaten its position as the industry leader. It soon became evident that consumers loved what Apple had created, and BlackBerry's market share fell over time from 50 percent to less than 1 percent.[24]

Productive obsession is not focused on the status quo but on striving to create something better for customers and society at large. The problem with many companies is that they obsess, if at all, on their existing business model, striving to improve current products and services, which will become obsolete. Barnes & Noble striving to make its bookstores more appealing with features such as coffee bars was not going to stop the onslaught that was Amazon. Sustaining the status quo can work for a while, but most industries undergo changes that require a more radical approach at certain points. A recent example is Netflix. The company effectively managed to grow its DVD-by-mail business, while simultaneously building its online streaming business—which became the source of its extraordinary growth. Uber will face a similar challenge in building a company that today has millions of drivers while transitioning to a future that will be heavily influenced by autonomous vehicles.

A second organizational pitfall is obsessing on growth at all costs. As discussed in chapter 5, Travis Kalanick fixated on growing Uber faster than its competition and aggressively opposed anyone who stood in his way. He did so because the firm with the most riders will, all things being equal, attract the most drivers and provide the fastest pickup times. This attracts even more riders and results in a self-generating momentum. Uber's "juicing growth" strategy resulted in it becoming the largest and most valuable ride-sharing service in the United States.

Uber is not alone in aggressively focusing on growth. Facebook is the preeminent social media site, with over two billion users world-wide.[25] The company has recently encountered a series of setbacks due to how it managed user data, including a failure to rigorously monitor third-party vendors. It also came under criticism as rogue operators, including foreign governments, used its service in unethical ways to influence public opinion and voting behavior in national elections.[26] It appears that individuals and countries were "weaponizing" Facebook through propaganda and fake news sent to targeted populations using

Facebook's tools. The company has taken steps to correct these failures through tighter controls and increased staffing to prevent and catch unethical behavior. However, one has to wonder if Facebook's unrelenting drive to grow and its business model based on selling user data were at least partially responsible for the problems that have plagued the firm.[27]

Equally problematic is when a firm obsesses on profit, viewing it as more important than customers and products. Some leaders drive their company on a quarter-to-quarter basis to deliver the numbers. They can't see beyond the next earnings call. Profit is clearly important at least over the long-term, but it can't become more important than developing great products and services. Steve Jobs believed that the way to ruin a growing firm is to put leaders in charge who care primarily about financial results:

> I have my own theory about why decline happens at companies. When the sales guys run the company, the product guys don't matter so much, and a lot of them just turn off. It happened at Apple when Sculley came in, which was my fault, and it happened when Ballmer took over at Microsoft.[28]

A different type of organizational pitfall occurs when leaders believe their role is to make their colleagues comfortable. Even more, some leaders design their company practices and culture to cater to their least-obsessive colleagues. In these cases, comfort and work-life balance take priority over striving to create a product or service that customers want. Some firms tell colleagues that they can't email about work-related issues past a specific time of day or over the weekend. They also don't want them, through their excessive work habits, to put pressure on their peers to do the same. Leaders and firms who emphasize work-life balance believe that it results in better work and the ability to attract and retain the best talent. In other words, people with the most talent often have a choice where they want to work and will choose those firms that provide a higher quality of life over those who demand too much.

It is hard to argue against work-life balance—but its unintended consequences also need to be considered. One argument is that work-life balance is both morally right and ultimately more productive. Arianna Huffington makes such a claim when she observes that tired and burned-out people make poor decisions.[29] That is certainly true in the extreme, but it is also true that companies with people who are completely committed to delivering something exceptional will generally outperform companies whose people go home at 5:00 p.m. each day. The question is, What is the right balance between these extremes for each company in general and particularly at critical points in its history?

Most would agree that extremes, where work is either all-important or unimportant, are problematic. However, determining the appropriate middle ground is the subject of ongoing debate and experimentation. Some firms expect people to respond to important issues at any waking hour, including late at night, weekends, and during vacations. Others limit, or at least discourage, people from working past regular hours or over weekends and holidays. These firms don't want people to neglect other areas of their life or act in ways that encourage others to neglect life outside of work (such as by emailing at all hours). Other firms, such as Tesla, would find this type of restriction ludicrous, believing it undermines effective outcomes and may even create more stress than it eliminates. Leaders such as Bezos and Musk are unapologetic about setting exacting standards and will quickly admit that working for their company is not for everyone. They are clear with potential hires about their performance-driven culture and the demands placed on employees. Tesla, for example, tells potential hires that they will be asked to work long hours and over some weekends. They want to be honest about the firm's expectations and work culture.

An indication that a company has gone too far in its demands is when individuals, particularly talented individuals, no longer want to work for it. They may find the work environment too stressful or the demands on their personal life too great. They may favor working for a firm that provides a more supportive environment, with a highly collaborative culture and shared accountability. Google is rated year after year as one of the best places to work, in part because of its team-based culture and the support it provides employees. While there are individuals who don't want to work for firms such as Amazon, Tesla, or Uber, each company continues to attract a large number of job applicants. Some of these firms, Apple and Amazon in particular, also engender a high level of colleague loyalty. Steve Jobs, given his demanding style, was asked if he was too tough on his team members. He said, "I don't think I run roughshod over people but if something sucks, I tell people to their face. It's my job to be honest."[30] He hired highly talented people who could work anywhere in the tech industry —but most wanted to continue working for him at Apple.

The problem with a comfort mentality is that it can shelter people from the realities of needing to perform at a high level. Paul Allen describes in his biography what it took to establish a firm that would eventually dominate its industry:

> We worked all hours, with double shifts on weekends. Bill basically stopped going to class. . . . I neglected my job at Honeywell, dragging into the office at noon. I'd stay until 5:30, and then it was back to Aiken until three or so in the morning. I'd save my files, crash for five or six hours, and start over. . . . I'd occasionally catch Bill grabbing naps at his terminal during our late-nighters. He'd be in the middle of a line of code when he'd gradually tilt forward until his nose touched the keyboard. After dozing for an hour or two, he'd open his eyes, squint at the screen, blink twice,

and resume precisely where he'd left off—a prodigious feat of concentration.[31]

A comfort mentality can also impact management practices. There is a growing body of research that suggests psychological safety is a critical aspect of high-performing teams and organizations. Amy Edmondson, a professor at Harvard, describes psychological safety as "a team climate characterized by interpersonal trust and mutual respect in which people are comfortable being themselves . . . a sense of confidence that the team will not embarrass, reject or punish someone for speaking up."[32] A psychologically safe culture is better able to learn and adapt than those lacking this cultural trait. That said, those embracing psychological safety must also recognize the possibility of unintended consequences.

Advocates of psychological safety maintain that it results in greater creativity and more candor, because the environment is more accepting of divergent views and, as a result, enhances learning and effective decision-making. However, this can easily become a culture where people are leery of challenging each other because they don't want to be seen as closed-minded, uncollaborative, or disrespectful.[33] A culture designed to promote more honest dialogue, ironically, can result in less honest dialogue. This is not the intent of those promoting psychological safety, but it can be the outcome.

I doubt that Steve Jobs or Elon Musk would warm to the idea of psychological safety. Jobs believed in the merits of aggressively challenging people when their ideas or products were unexceptional. He said, "My job is not to be easy on people. My job is to make them better,"[34] adding, "My job is to say when something sucks rather than sugarcoat it."[35] His focus was not on the team members' feelings but on the quality of the product they were producing. Most understood that was the price of admission for working with Jobs and remained loyal to him.

Jobs also believed that team members needed to be tough on each other. He told of an experience he had as a child living near an elderly man who owned a rock tumbler. One day, Jobs and his neighbor found some rocks in the backyard and put them in the tumbler, along with grit powder and liquid. As the stones started banging against each other in the tumbler, Jobs's neighbor told him to come back the next day. Jobs returned to find the stones transformed.

> Through rubbing up against each other, creating a little bit of friction, creating a little bit of noise, had come out these beautiful polished rocks. And that has always been my metaphor for a team working really hard on something that they are passionate about. That it is through the team, through that group of incredibly talented people bumping up against each other having arguments, having fights sometimes and making noise, and working together they polish each other and they polish the ideas and what comes out are these really beautiful stones.[36]

THE OBSESSIVE IMPERATIVE

A risk, then, for organizations is becoming soft and complacent as they grow. A related risk is that they become distracted from what matters most. Michael Moritz, who leads a private equity firm with a history of investing in successful start-up companies, notes that the US in general, and Silicon Valley in particular, is becoming preoccupied with concerns that result in a loss of focus. He writes that in some prominent firms,

> there have been complaints about the political sensibilities of speakers invited to address a corporate audience; debates over the appropriate length of paternity leave or work-life balances; and grumbling about the need for a space for

musical jam sessions. These seem like the concerns of a society that is becoming unhinged.[37]

Moritz believes companies with a clear focus and strong work ethic will outpace others. He describes the intense drive he sees in Chinese firms providing a stark contrast to what is becoming the norm in some US firms. This is not to suggest that companies should embrace a harsh work environment or ignore larger social issues and needs. Nor should they deviate in any way from doing the right thing. But companies, particularly successful companies, are always in danger of becoming distracted and allowing peripheral concerns to become more important than their customers and products.

Obsession is an antidote to complacency and distraction.[38] However, obsession's dark side presents a different type of risk to organizations. Good and bad often exist in close proximity in obsessed leaders and teams—they are inseparably bound together. Those who can achieve the extraordinary are also those with the potential to do great damage. The easy resolution of this contradiction is to not hire customer or product obsessives, or to restrict their behavior to the point that they are no longer a threat. That approach works only in a business environment that is free of disruptive forces—and there are fewer of those industries with each passing year.

Today, there are an estimated seventy thousand abandoned buildings in Detroit, with the largest being the Packard Car plant that closed in 1958.[39] Buildings on that industrial site are now in a state of disrepair and many are covered with graffiti.[40] The plant was even used by a filmmaker seeking to portray an apocalyptic world. Many factors contributed to Detroit's deterioration and eventual bankruptcy, but a primary factor was the decline of the major US auto manufacturers—GM, Chrysler, and Ford. In the 1960s, the Big Three's US market share was above 85 percent. By 2008, it was 44 percent—a precipitous fall that had widespread economic and social consequences in Detroit and beyond.[41] Leadership in those companies failed their employees, their communities, and their shareholders. They made many mistakes but perhaps the most egregious was designing and manufacturing shoddy products.[42] They lost sight of the need to build reliable and compelling cars that people wanted to buy. These companies were run for decades by leaders with finance and business backgrounds, men who were not product visionaries.[43] Elon Musk, in spite of his highly publicized missteps, has done what the US auto companies failed to do for fifty years—bring to market a boldly innovative car that is far superior to its competition. Companies without obsessives, resolutely focused on what truly matters, lack what is needed to thrive in a highly volatile world. All told, we need obsession because fortune favors the obsessed.

TAKEAWAYS

- Organizations are ambivalent about obsession, given its potential for good and bad. They want what obsession provides but also recognize its significant downsides.
- Savvy organizational design and management can maximize obsession's positives while minimizing its risks. This includes decisions around a firm's mission, structure, and people.
- Well-designed safeguards are essential but should not be so restrictive that they undermine obsession's role in producing products and services that customers value.
- Organizations also need to be careful that they don't become distracted from their primary purpose—and, in so doing, fail to sustain the all-consuming focus and unrelenting drive needed to achieve the extraordinary.

NOTES

Chapter One: Going All In

1. Quote attributed to M. Cobanli. Cited by Carlos Alvarenga in his post "Corporate Personalities: The Good, The Bad and The Ugly," LinkedIn, March 23, 2019, https://www.linkedin.com/pulse/corporate-personalities-good-bad-ugly-carlos-alvarenga/. Also see Frank Scott, "Good vs Great Design Quotes," Design.Amid, June 26, 2014, http://www.designamid.com/magazine.php?pageno=313.

2. Warren Buffet said of Jeff Bezos, "To succeed in two different big businesses in a huge way, I can't think of another example like it." Jonathan Vanian, "Warren Buffet Praises Amazon and Jeff Bezos While Selling IBM Shares," *Fortune*, May 5, 2017, http://fortune.com/2017/05/05/warren-buffett-amazon-bezos-ibm/. He also noted, "I've never seen any person develop two really important industries at the same time and really be the operational guy in both." Tae Kim, "Warren Buffett on Amazon Cloud's Success: 'You Do Not Want to Give Jeff Bezos a 7-Year Head Start,'" CNBC, May 15, 2018, https://www.cnbc.com/2018/05/15/warren-buffett-on-amazons-cloud-success-you-do-not-want-to-give-jeff-bezos-a-7-year-head-start.html. Some would argue that Steve Jobs transformed four industries: computers (Mac), telecommunications (iPhone), music (Apple streaming), and animation movies (Pixar).

3. Amazon Prime now delivers thousands of its products in one or two hours in some US cities.

4. Jeff Holden, who worked for Bezos at D. E. Shaw & Co. and later at Amazon, says Bezos was "the most introspective guy I ever met. He was very methodical about everything in his life." *Bezos and the Age of Amazon* (New York: Little, Brown & Company, 2014), 21.

5. The original name of Amazon was Cadabra. Bezos also considered Awake.com, Browse.com, Bookmall.com, and Aard.com. Dave Smith, "Jeff Bezos Almost Gave Amazon a Different Name," *Business Insider*, January 22, 2016, www.businessinsider.com/jeff-bezos-amazon-name-alternatives-2016-1.

6. Jodi Kantor and David Streitfeld, "Inside Amazon: Wrestling Big Ideas in a Bruising Workplace," *New York Times*, August 15, 2015, https://www.nytimes.com/2015/08/16/technology/inside-amazon-wrestling-big-ideas-in-a-bruising-workplace.html.

7. J. Clement, "Most Popular Retail Websites in the United States as of December 2018, Ranked by Visitors (in Millions)," Statista, July 23, 2019, https://www.statista.com/statistics/271450/monthly-unique-visitors-to-us-retail-websites/.

8. Justin Dallaire, "Amazon Ranked Most Trusted E-Commerce Retailer," Strategy, July 18, 2018, http://strategyonline.ca/2018/07/18/amazon-ranked-canadas-most-trusted-ecommerce-retailer/.

9.   The engineer also noted that this hypothetical alien, in addition to being highly intelligent, had only a tangential interest in human affairs.

10. Steve Yegge, "Googler Steve Yegge Apologizes for Platform Rant, Shares Bezos War Story," Launch, October 21, 2011, https://launch.co/blog/googler-steve-yegge-apologizes-for-platform-rant-shares-bezo.html.

11. Amy Martinez, "Bezos Credits Amazon's Success to Luck, Good Timing," *Seattle Times*, January 15, 2013, https://www.seattletimes.com/business/bezos-credits-amazonrsquos-success-to-luck-good-timing/.

12. Warren St. John, "Barnes & Noble's Epiphany," Wired, June 1, 1999, https://www.wired.com/1999/06/barnes-2/.

13. Bezos noted he was even luckier because he had a seven-year head start on other technology companies when he launched Amazon Web Services. The established tech firms, such as Microsoft and IBM, underestimated the threat that Bezos and Amazon posed as a competitor.

14. Research by Charles A. O'Reilly and his colleagues demonstrates the impact of a CEO's personality on the values and behaviors of a firm, as well as its financial performance. See O'Reilly et al., "The Promise and Problems of Organizational Culture: CEO Personality, Culture, and Firm Performance," *Group and Organization Management* 39, no. 6 (September 2014): 595–624.

15. "All Achievers: Jeffrey P. Bezos," Academy of Achievement, August 22, 2019, http://www.achievement.org/achiever/jeffrey-p-bezos/.

16. Brad Stone, *The Everything Store: Jeff Bezos and the Age of Amazon* (New York: Little, Brown & Company, 2013), loc. 330, Kindle.

17. Phil LeBeau, "This Is the Best Car Consumer Reports Has Ever Tested," CNBC, August 27, 2015, https://www.cnbc.com/2015/08/27/teslas-p85d-is-the-best-car-consumer-reports-has-ever-tested.html.

18. "Tesla Model S Achieves Best Safety Rating of Any Car Ever Tested," Tesla, August 19, 2013, https://www.tesla.com/it_IT/blog/Tesla-model-s-achieves-best-safety-rating-any-car-ever-tested.

19. I. Wagner, "Number of Tesla Vehicles Delivered Worldwide from 3rd Quarter 2015 to 2nd Quarter 2019," Statista, July 22, 2019, https://www.statista.com/statistics/502208/tesla-quarterly-vehicle-deliveries/; https://electrek.co/2018/11/16/tesla-fleet-10-billion-electric-miles/.

20. Emily Chasan, "Tesla's First Impact Report Puts Hard Number on CO2 Emissions," Bloomberg, April 17, 2019, https://www.bloomberg.com/news/articles/2019-04-17/tesla-s-first-impact-report-puts-hard-number-on-co2-emissions.

21. Meghan Daum, "Elon Musk Wants to Change How (and Where) Humans Live," *Vogue*, September 21, 2015, https://www.vogue.com/article/elon-musk-profile-entrepreneur-spacex-tesla-motors.

22. *Online Etymology Dictionary*, s.v. "Obsession (n.)," accessed October 23, 2019, https://www.etymonline.com/word/obsession.

23. Productive obsession, as defined in this book, is a desirable and often pleasurable fixation. In addition, when properly focused and managed, productive obsessions can contribute to the well-being of organizations and society at large.

24. Gary Thomson, "She Was a Chronicler of Our Times," *Philadelphia Inquirer*, June 23, 2019.

25. Her archive is being digitized for those wanting to research the history of television. Strokes's obsessive taping of news shows may yet prove to be of value.

26. Eric Maisel uses the term "productive obsession" in his book *Brainstorm: Harnessing the Power of Productive Obsessions* (Novato, CA: New World Library, 2010), i.

27. Justine Musk, "How Can I Be as Great as Bill Gates, Steve Jobs, Elon Musk or Sir Richard Branson?," Quora, September 12, 2017, https://www.quora.com/How -can-I-be-as-great-as-Bill-Gates-Steve-Jobs-Elon-Musk-or-Sir-Richard-Branson /answer/Justine-Musk?share=1&srid=iAix.

28. Lennard J. Davis, *Obsession: A History* (Chicago: University of Chicago Press, 2009), 27. G. W. F. Hegel wrote the following passage about passion: "We assert then that nothing has been accomplished without an interest on the part of those who brought it about. And if 'interest' be called 'passion'—because the whole individuality is concentrating all its desires and powers, with every fiber of volition, to the neglect of all other actual or possible interests and aims, on one object—we may then affirm without qualification that nothing great in the world has been accomplished without passion." Georg Wilhelm Friedrich Hegel, *Reason In History: A General Introduction to the Philosophy of History*, trans. Robert S. Hartman (Indianapolis: Liberal Arts Press Book, 1953), https://www.marxists.org/reference/archive/hegel/works/hi/introduction.htm.

29. Davis, *Obsession*, 18.

30. See David McCullough, *The Great Bridge: The Epic Story of the Building of the Brooklyn Bridge* (New York: Simon & Schuster, 1972). Construction began in 1869 and was completed in 1883.

31. This is not to suggest that building bridges always requires the Roeblings' level of sacrifice. That said, the human cost that comes with creating something extraordinary is often more extreme than most realize. Another case study in obsessive genius is Marie Curie, who won two Nobel prizes for her scientific work. Her life was one of personal sacrifices, including decades of exposure to radioactive materials that likely resulted in her death.

32. Maya Salam, "Overlooked No More: Alison Hargreaves, Who Conquered Everest Solo and Without Bottled Oxygen," *New York Times*, June 12, 2018, https://www.nytimes.com/2018/03/14/obituaries/overlooked-alison -hargreaves.html.

33. Hargreaves's son, Thomas Ballard, was climbing mountains before he was born, as his mother made a difficult climb in the Alps when she was six months pregnant. Thomas became a highly accomplished mountain climber, including being the first person to climb the six great north faces in the Alps during the winter. His mother was the first person to do so in the summer, twenty-three years before her son. At the age of thirty, Thomas died while summitting Nanga Parbat in Pakistan.

34. Salam, "Overlooked No More."

35. One of the most famous expressions of this belief is found in Herman Melville's novel *Moby Dick*. Captain Ahab tells a member of his crew who questions his

obsessive quest to kill the great white whale, "Ahab is for ever Ahab, man. This whole act's immutably decreed. 'Twas rehearsed by thee and me a billion years before this ocean rolled. Fool! I am the Fates' lieutenant, I act under orders."

36. Another example of an obsessive personality in the climbing world is Alex Honnold. After years of planning and forty roped climbs of Yosemite's El Capitan, he made the first free solo ascent of the famous rock face—climbing the nearly 3,000-foot granite wall without ropes or other safety gear. A fall on the rock face would have resulted in his certain death.

37. Ian MacKinnon, "Mountain Heroine Feared Dead," *Independent*, August 15, 1995.

38. Timothy B. Lee, "The Secrets to Elon Musk's Success," *Vox*, April 10, 2017, https://www.vox.com/new-money/2017/4/10/15211542/elon-musk-success-secret.

39. Grace Reader, "19 Times Elon Musk Had the Best Response," *Entrepreneur*, February 23, 2018, https://www.entrepreneur.com/article/277986.

40. The employment figure is for the US alone. Thousands more work for Apple worldwide, including large suppliers operating primarily in China. See Apple Inc., "Apple's US Job Footprint Grows to 2.4 Million," Apple Newsroom, August 15, 2019, https://www.apple.com/newsroom/2019/08/apples-us-job-footprint-grows -to-two-point-four-million/.

41. Nathan Heller, "Naked Launch," *New Yorker*, November 25, 2013, https://www .newyorker.com/magazine/2013/11/25/naked-launch.

42. See Walter Isaacson, *Steve Jobs* (New York: Simon & Schuster, 2011).

43. Apple has struggled since Jobs's death to develop highly innovative products. Some believe CEO Tim Cook, with a background in operations, lacks a necessary product obsession. This may be the case even as Apple continues to grow and financially perform well—sustaining itself primarily on the products developed during Jobs's tenure while expanding into a variety of profitable service offerings.

44. Heller, "Launch."

45. The novelist Marie von Ebner-Eschenbach wrote, "He who believes in freedom of the will has never loved and never hated." *Aphorisms* (Riverside, CA: Ariadne Press, 1994), 22.

Chapter Two: Beyond Grit

1. Angela Lee Duckworth, *Grit: The Power of Passion and Perseverance* (New York: Scribner, 2016). See also Angela Lee Duckworth et al., "Deliberate Practice Spells Success: Why Grittier Competitors Triumph at the National Spelling Bee," *Social Psychological and Personality Science* 2, no. 2 (October 2010): 174–81.

2. Shankar Vedantam, "The Power and Problem of Grit," NPR, April 5, 2016, https://www.npr.org/2016/04/04/472162167/the-power-and-problem-of-grit.

3. The grit research is criticized by some on both technical and philosophical grounds. See M. Credé, M. C. Tynan, and P. D. Harms, "Much Ado About Grit: A Meta-Analytic Synthesis of the Grit Literature," *Journal of Personality and Social Psychology* 113, no. 3 (2017): 492–511.

4. Angela Duckworth, "Q&A," https://angeladuckworth.com/qa/. A study indicates that gritty individuals will sometimes persevere when they should quit (in

pursuing a losing proposition). See G. Lucas et al., "When the Going Gets Tough: Grit Predicts Costly Perseverance," *Journal of Research in Personality* 59 (2015).

5. Duckworth, "Q&A."

6. Emma Johnson, "Elon Musk Wants to Save the World—At What Cost?," *Success*, August 7, 2017, https://www.success.com/elon-musk-wants-to-save-the-world-at -what-cost/.

7. "Obsession," Dictionary.com, https://www.dictionary.com/browse/obsession.

8. Judd Biasiotto and Richard Williams, "The Soul of a Champion: Part 1," Magnus ver Magnússon, May 27, 2010, http://magnusvermagnusson.com/?p=408.

9. Most believe his record of 262 hits in one season, achieved in 2004 as a Seattle Mariner, will never be equaled.

10. Pete Rose holds the record for hits in Major League Baseball because Ichiro's hits in Japan are not included in its statistics. Rose argues that to do so would be the equivalent of counting minor league hits in the MLB records.

11. Wright Thompson, "When Winter Never Ends," *ESPN Magazine*, March 7, 2018, http://www.espn.com/espn/feature/story/_/id/22624561/ichiro-suzuki-return -seattle-mariners-resolve-internal-battle.

12. David Foster Wallace, "The String Theory," *Esquire*, September 17, 2008, https://www.esquire.com/sports/a5151/the-string-theory-david-foster-wallace/.

13. Wallace, "String Theory."

14. Jonah Weiner, "Jerry Seinfeld Intends to Die Standing Up," *New York Times*, December 20, 2012, https://www.nytimes.com/2012/12/23/magazine/jerry -seinfeld-intends-to-die-standing-up.html.

15. Weiner, "Jerry Seinfeld."

16. Cleveland Moffitt, "A Talk With Tesla," *Atlanta Constitution*, June 7, 1896, https://wist.info/tesla-nikola/18326/.

17. Mark McGuinness, *Motivation for Creative People: How to Stay Creative While Gaining Money* (n.p.: Lateral Action Books, 2015). Another story illustrating Kubrick's obsessive personality describes him preparing for a movie about Napoleon. With his assistant, they compiled twenty-five thousand index cards with information about the French leader and his family. The movie never made it to production.

18. Elon Musk is also known to make unreasonable requests. For example, his SpaceX team designed space suits for human flight to the International Space Station and, eventually, Mars. Musk wanted the suits to be technically superior but also more streamlined and appealing than those then worn by American and Russian astronauts.

19. Andrew Chaikin, "Is SpaceX Changing the Rocket Equation?," *Air and Space Magazine*, January 2012, https://www.airspacemag.com/space/is-spacex -changing-the-rocket-equation-132285884/.

20. Chaikin, "SpaceX."

21. "All Achievers: Jeffrey P. Bezos," Academy of Achievement.

22. Jon Jachimowicz and Sam McNerney, "The Problem with Following Your Passion," *Washington Post*, November 6, 2015, https://www.washingtonpost.com /news/on-leadership/wp/2015/11/06/the-problem-with-following-your-passion/.

23. Carl Hoffman, "Now 0-for-3, Space X's Elon Musk Vows to Make Orbit," Wired, August 5, 2008, https://www.wired.com/2008/08/musk-qa/.

24. Emily Shanklin, "NASA Selects SpaceX's Falcon 9 Booster and Dragon Spacecraft for Cargo Resupply," SpaceX (website), December 23, 2008, https://www.spacex.com/PRESS/2012/12/19/NASA-SELECTS-SPACEXS-FALCON-9-BOOSTER-AND-DRAGON-SPACECRAFT-CARGO-RESUPPLY.

25. Marina Krakovsky, "Why Mindset Matters," *Stanford Magazine*, September 20, 2017, https://medium.com/stanford-magazine/carol-dweck-mindset-research-eb80831095b5.

26. Inspired Action, "Elon Musk, Interview with Danish TV, 27th September, 2015," YouTube video, 12:15, September 30, 2015, https://www.youtube.com/watch?v=rdCkDSXQC1Q&feature=youtu.be.

27. Emma Seppata and Julia Moeller, "1 in 5 Employees Is Highly Engaged and at Risk of Burnout," *Harvard Business Review*, February 2, 2018, https://hbr.org/2018/02/1-in-5-highly-engaged-employees-is-at-risk-of-burnout.

28. In a different study, many who worked excessive hours showed fewer signs of physical stress if they were fully engaged with their work. See L. Brummelhuis et al., "Beyond Nine to Five: Is Working to Excess Bad for Health?," *Academy of Management Discoveries* 3, no. 3 (September 2017), https://journals.aom.org/doi/10.5465/amd.2017.0120.

29. Lieke ten Brummelhuis and Nancy P. Rothbard, "How Being a Workaholic Differs from Working Long Hours—And Why That Matters to Your Health," *Harvard Business Review*, March 22, 2018, https://hbr.org/2018/03/how-being-a-workaholic-differs-from-working-long-hours-and-why-that-matters-for-your-health.

30. Davis, *Obsession: A History*.

31. These are the Grant and Glueck studies at Harvard.

32. Randall Graham, a winemaker in California, has dedicated his life to producing new varietals of wine that are of world-class quality. He noted, "I know perfectly well that there are elements in my character that have isolated me from people . . . that the intensity of my obsessions often crowds out the expression of my affections. There's no one in the world I love more than my daughter, but I struggle to explain the importance of all this to her." Adam Gopnik, "A Vintner's Quest to Create a Truly American Wine," *New Yorker*, May 14, 2018, https://www.newyorker.com/magazine/2018/05/21/a-vintners-quest-to-create-a-truly-american-wine.

33. There is debate on the actual divorce rate in the US, with some suggesting it is much lower than the often-cited 50 percent figure. See Virginia Pelly, "What Is the Divorce Rate in America?," Fatherly, May 22, 2019, https://www.fatherly.com/love-money/what-is-divorce-rate-america/.

34. Musk said, "I would like to allocate more time to dating, though. I need to find a girlfriend. That's why I need to carve out just a little more time. I think maybe even another five to ten—how much time does a woman want a week? Maybe ten hours? That's kind of the minimum? I don't know." Bill Murphy Jr., "27 Elon

Musk Quotes That Will Very Likely Change How You Feel about Elon Musk," *Inc.*, September 8, 2019, https://www.inc.com/bill-murphy-jr/27-elon-musk -quotes-that-will-very-likely-change-how-you-feel-about-elon-musk.html.

35. An estimated one million people worldwide are killed in cars each year, and twenty to fifty million are injured. "Road Traffic Injuries," World Health Organization, December 7, 2018, https://www.who.int/news-room/fact-sheets /detail/road-traffic-injuries.

36. Burkhard Bilger, "Autocorrect," *New Yorker*, November 25, 2013, https://www .newyorker.com/magazine/2013/11/25/auto-correct.

37. Bilger.

38. Charles Duhigg, "Did Uber Steal Google's Intellectual Property?," *New Yorker*, October 15, 2018, https://www.newyorker.com/magazine/2018/10/22/did-uber -steal-googles-intellectual-property.

39. Guy Kawasaki, "Guy Kawasaki: At Apple, 'You Had to Prove Yourself Every Day, or Steve Jobs Got Rid of You,'" CNBC, March 1, 2019, https://www.cnbc .com/2019/03/01/former-apple-employee-guy-kawasaki-once-stood-up-to-steve -jobs-here-is-the-amazing-response-he-received.html.

40. Ben Austen, "The Story of Steve Jobs: An Inspiration or a Cautionary Tale?," *Wired*, July 23, 2012, https://www.wired.com/2012/07/ff_stevejobs/.

41. Walter Isaacson, "Walter Isaacson Talks Steve Jobs," Commonwealth Club, December 14, 2011, https://www.commonwealthclub.org/events/archive /transcript/walter-isaacson-talks-steve-jobs.

42. Nicholas Hune-Brown, "The Genius, Obsession and Cruelty of Amazon's Jeff Bezos," Canadian Business, November 14, 2013, https://www.canadianbusiness. com/technology-news/the-genius-obsession-and-cruelty-of-amazons-jeff-bezos/.

43. Stone, *Everything Store*, 178.

44. Yegge, "Googler Steve Yegge Apologizes for Platform Rant, Shares Bezos War Story," *Launch*, October 21, 2011, https://launch.co/blog/googler-steve-yegge -apologizes-for-platform-rant-shares-bezo.html.

45. Mark Abadi, "Jeff Bezos Once Said That in Job Interviews He Told Candidates of 3 Ways to Work—and That You Have to Do All 3 at Amazon," *Business Insider*, August 12, 2018, https://www.businessinsider.com/jeff-bezos-amazon -employees-work-styles-2018-8.

46. There is a long-standing debate on means versus end when it comes to how we treat others. Immanuel Kant wrote, "Act in such a way that you treat humanity, whether in your own person or in the person of another, always at the same time as an end and never simply as a means." *Groundwork of Metaphysic of Morals*, ed. and trans. Allen W. Wood (New Haven, CT: Yale University Press, 2002), 19. Some of the leaders profiled in this book would fall short if held to that standard.

47. Austen, "Story of Steve Jobs."

48. Austen.

49. Liam Tung, "Microsoft's Bill Gates: Steve Jobs Cast Spells on Everyone but He Didn't Fool Me," ZDNet, July 8, 2019, https://www.zdnet.com/article /microsofts-bill-gates-steve-jobs-cast-spells-on-everyone-but-he-didnt-fool-me/.

50. Linux Kernel, "Code of Conflict," https://www.kernel.org/doc/html/v4.17 /process/code-of-conflict.html.

51. Noam Cohen, "After Years of Abusive E-mails, the Creator of Linux Steps Aside," *New Yorker*, September 19, 2019, https://www.newyorker.com/science /elements/after-years-of-abusive-e-mails-the-creator-of-linux-steps-aside.

52. Cohen, "After Years of Abusive E-mails." A professor at Rutgers University who specializes in human resource management writes, "We'd love to find out if there are good aspects of abusive leadership. There's been a lot of research. We just can't find any upside." Quoted in Cary Benedict, "When the Bully is the Boss," *New York Times*, February 26, 2019, https://www.nytimes. com/2019/02/26/health/boss-bullies-workplace-management.html.

53. Lorraine Lorenzo, "Tesla Trouble Continues as Head of Production Quits," International Business Times, June 28, 2019, https://www.ibtimes.com/tesla -trouble-continues-head-production-quits-2803513. See also Dana Hull, "'There's Something Wrong': Tesla's Rapid Executive Turnover Raises Eyebrows as Musk Thins the Ranks," *Financial Post*, May 14, 2018, https://business. financialpost.com/transportation/autos/theres-something-wrong-rapid-tesla -executive-turnover-raises-eyebrows-as-musk-thins-the-ranks.

54. Shankar Vedantam, "The Scarcity Trap—Why We Keep Digging When We're Stuck in a Hole," NPR, April 2, 2018, https://www.npr.org/2017/03/20 /520587241/the-scarcity-trap-why-we-keep-digging-when-were-stuck-in-a -hole.

55. Vedantam, "Scarcity Trap."

56. Sendhil Mullainathan and Eldar Shafir, *Scarcity: Why Having Too Little Means So Much* (New York: Times Books, 2013), 24.

57. Mullainathan and Shafir, *Scarcity*, 29.

58. The tunnel vision of obsessive personalities can also mean that larger concerns are minimized in the pursuit of one's goal. Joan Didion authored insightful novels and essays about American society. In a documentary about her life, she described an experience when she was writing a piece about the counterculture in San Francisco in the 1960s. She went to a house where she met a five-year-old child who was on acid. An interviewer asked her decades later what is was like as a journalist to see a child on drugs. Her response was, "Let me tell you, it was gold. I mean, that's the long and short of it . . . you live for moments like that . . . if you're . . . doing a piece." *Joan Didion: The Center Will Not Hold*, directed by Griffin Dunne (Los Gatos, CA: Netflix, 2017).

59. Musk's ability to build a high-performance organization is evident at SpaceX, where there is less controversy, lower turnover, and a positive culture.

60. Jason Roberson, "Jeff, Welcome to Dallas," *Dallas Business Journal*, April 23, 2018, https://www.bizjournals.com/dallas/news/2018/04/23/amazon-jeff-bezos-dallas -bush-institute.html.

61. Alexander Nazaryan, "How Jeff Bezos Is Hurtling Toward World Domination," *Newsweek*, July 12, 2016, https://www.newsweek.com/2016/07/22/jeff-bezos -amazon-ceo-world-domination-479508.html.

62. Nikola Tesla, "The Problem of Increasing Human Energy," *Century Magazine*, June 1900, 175–211, https://teslauniverse.com/nikola-tesla/articles/problem -increasing-human-energy.

63. Henry Blodget, "The Maturation of the Billionaire Boy-Man," *New York Magazine*, May 6, 2012, http://nymag.com/news/features/mark-zuckerberg-2012-5/; Charles Arthur, "Facebook Paid Up to $65m to Founder Mark Zuckerberg's Ex-Classmates," *The Guardian*, February 12, 2009, https://www.theguardian.com /technology/2009/feb/12/facebook-mark-zuckerberg-ex-classmates.

64. In a movie about Facebook, the character playing Zuckerberg tells those who are suing him, "If you guys were the inventors of Facebook, you would have invented Facebook." *The Social Network*, directed by David Fincher (Culver City, CA: Sony Pictures, 2010).

65. Paul Allen, *Idea Man* (New York: Penguin Group, 2011), 32.

66. Allen, *Idea Man*, 165.

Chapter Three: Delighting Customers

1. Shep Hyken, "Amazon: The Most Convenient Store On The Planet," *Forbes*, July 22, 2018, https://www.forbes.com/sites/shephyken/2018/07/22/amazon-the -most-convenient-store-on-the-planet/#8d1340e1e98f.

2. Alina Selyukh, "What Americans Told Us About Online Shopping Says a Lot About Amazon," NPR, June 6, 2018, https://www.npr.org/2018/06/06/615137239 /what-americans-told-us-about-online-shopping-says-a-lot-about-amazon.

3. Selyukh, "What Americans Told Us."

4. Hyken, "Amazon."

5. Arjun Kharpal, "Amazon Is Not a Monopoly, but There's No Question Why It's So Dominant, Tech Investor Palihapitiya Says," CNBC, December 12, 2017, https://www.cnbc.com/2017/12/12/amazon-is-a-natural-product-monopoly -venture-capitalist-palihapitiya-says.html.

6. Revenue in 1996 was just over $2.448 billion. Barnes & Noble Inc., *1998 Annual Report*, http://www.annualreports.com/HostedData/AnnualReportArchive/b /NYSE_BKS_1998.pdf.

7. Revenue in 1996 was $15.746 million. Amazon.com, Inc., *Form 10-K for the Year Ended December 31, 1997*, accessed October 23, 2019, https://ir.aboutamazon.com /static-files/430df638-b327-42d8-9c9f-7f5101962ba2.

8. Stone, *Everything Store*, 57.

9. The "Amazon.toast" statement was made by Forrester Research chief George Colony.

10. Julia Kirby and Thomas A. Stewart, "The Institutional Yes," *Harvard Business Review*, October 10, 2007, https://hbr.org/2007/10/the-institutional-yes.

11. See Jeff Bezos, "Letter to Shareholders," 1998, http://media.corporate-ir.net /media_files/irol/97/97664/reports/Shareholderletter98.pdf.

12. Bezos wrote: "As a company, one of our greatest cultural strengths is accepting the fact that if you're going to invent, you're going to disrupt. A lot of entrenched interests are not going to like it. Some of them will be genuinely concerned about the new way, and some of them will have a vested self-interest in preserving the old way. But in both cases, they're going to create a lot of noise, and it's very easy for employees to be

distracted by that." Steven Levy, "Jeff Bezos Owns the Web in More Ways Than You Think," *Wired*, November 13, 2011, https://www.wired.com/2011/11/ff_bezos/.

13. eMarketer Editors, "Digital Investments Pay Off for Walmart in Ecommerce Race," eMarketer, February 14, 2019, https://www.emarketer.com/content/digital-investments-pay-off-for-walmart-in-ecommerce-race.

14. "If You Had Invested Right After Amazon's IOP," Investopedia, May 5, 2019, https://www.investopedia.com/articles/investing/082715/if-you-had-invested-right-after-amazons-ipo.asp. The stock's climb has made Bezos, by some accounts, the richest person in the world. It also created approximately $850 billion in wealth for other investors.

15. "Barnes & Noble, Inc.," TheStreet, August 6, 2019, https://www.thestreet.com/quote/BKS.html.

16. Lizzy Gurdus, "Cramer Remix: Amazon Is the Death Star," CNBC, November 17, 2017, https://www.cnbc.com/2017/11/17/cramer-remix-amazon-is-the-death-star.html.

17. In 2015, Bezos was still repeating the customer-obsession theme evident in his first shareholder letter. He told a journalist, who was asking about Amazon's future plans to disrupt existing industries, "We don't seek to disrupt, we seek to delight." James Quinn, "Amazon's Jeff Bezos: With Jeremy Clarkson, We're Entering a New Golden Age of Television," *Telegraph*, August 16, 2015, https://www.telegraph.co.uk/technology/amazon/11800890/jeff-bezos-interview-amazon-prime-jeremy-clarkson.html.

18. Jeff Bezos, "2016 Letter to Shareholders," Amazon Blog, April 17, 2017, https://blog.aboutamazon.com/company-news/2016-letter-to-shareholders.

19. Jeff Bezos, "2017 Letter to Shareholders," Amazon Blog, April 18, 2018, https://blog.aboutamazon.com/company-news/2017-letter-to-shareholders/.

20. David LaGesse, "America's Best Leaders: Jeff Bezos, Amazon.com CEO," *US News & World Report*, November 19, 2008, https://www.usnews.com/news/best-leaders/articles/2008/11/19/americas-best-leaders-jeff-bezos-amazoncom-ceo.

21. Bill Murphy. I Ran the Full Text of Jeff Bezos's 23 Amazon Shareholder Letters Through a Word Cloud Generator, and the Insights Were Astonishing. *Inc.*, April 13, 2019, https://www.billmurphyjr.com@BillMurphyJr. "How Many Products Does Amazon Sell? April 2019," ScrapeHero, April 24, 2019, https://www.scrapehero.com/number-of-products-on-amazon-april-2019/.

22. "Customer Obsession: Leaders start with the customer and work backwards. They work vigorously to earn and keep customer trust. Although leaders pay attention to competitors, they obsess over customers." "Leadership Principles," Amazon Jobs, https://www.amazon.jobs/en/principles.

23. Bezos said, "Years from now, when people look back at Amazon, I want them to say that we uplifted customer-centricity across the entire business world. If we can do that, it will be really cool." Kirby and Stewart, "Institutional Yes."

24. Jim Collins, "How Does Your Flywheel Turn?," Jim Collins (website), https://www.jimcollins.com/tools/How-does-your-flywheel-turn.pdf.

25. Kirby and Stewart, "Institutional Yes."

26. Kirby and Stewart.

27. Jeff Dyer and Hal Gregersen, "How Does Amazon Stay At Day One?," *Forbes*, August 8, 2017, https://www.forbes.com/sites/innovatorsdna/2017/08/08/how-does-amazon-stay-at-day-one/#285b85147e4d.

28. Amazon's first book reviews were written by employees. The company then provided all customers with the opportunity to contribute feedback via reviews.

29. The patent expired in 2017. Mintz, Levin, Cohn, Ferris, Glovsky, and Popeo, P.C., "Have You Ever Used a One-Click Ordering Process Online? Then You Indirectly Paid Amazon," *The National Law Review*, January 8, 2018, https://www.natlawreview.com/article/have-you-ever-used-one-click-ordering-process-online-then-you-indirectly-paid-amazon.

30. The number of goals in 2010. See Jeff Bezos, "2009 Letter to Shareholders," Amazon.com, accessed October 24, 2019, https://ir.aboutamazon.com/static-files/54e35115-6b28-4227-aec1-6d31373cbd16. Each of Amazon's goals has an owner(s), specific deliverables, and target completion dates.

31. Levy, "Jeff Bezos Owns the Web."

32. The account of this meeting described Bezos as accusing the customer service leader of incompetence and lying. Stone, *Everything Store*, 113.

33. Bezos joked that Amazon started with the thought of being a small profitable business and grew to become a large and unprofitable business. See "Jeff Bezos," The Economic Club of Washington, DC, September 13, 2018, https://www.economicclub.org/events/jeff-bezos#targetText=The%20Economic%20Club%20of%20Washington%20celebrated%20many%20milestones%20on%20September,CEO%20and%20Founder%20of%20Amazon.

34. Kirby and Stewart, "Institutional Yes."

35. Kirby and Stewart.

36. As of 2014. See Amazon, "Amazon's Fulfillment Network," Amazon.com, accessed October 23, 2019, https://www.aboutamazon.com/working-at-amazon/amazons-fulfillment-network.

37. Stone, *Everything Store*, 327.

38. Stone, 325.

39. "Leadership Principles," Amazon Jobs.

40. Jeff Bezos, "2015 Letter to Shareholders," Amazon, https://ir.aboutamazon.com/static-files/f124548c-5d0b-41a6-a670-d85bb191fcec.

41. Laura Stevens, "Jeff Wilke: The Amazon Chief Who Obsesses Over Consumers," *Wall Street Journal*, October 11, 2017, https://www.wsj.com/articles/jeff-wilke-the-amazon-chief-who-obsesses-over-consumers-1507627802.

42. Mark Leibovich, "Child Prodigy, Online Pioneer," *Washington Post*, September 3, 2000, https://www.washingtonpost.com/archive/politics/2000/09/03/child-prodigy-online-pioneer/2ab207dc-d13a-4204-8949-493686e43415/.

43. Kirby and Stewart, "Institutional Yes."

44. Taylor Sopher, "'Failure and Innovation Are Inseparable Twins': Amazon Founder Jeff Bezos Offers 7 Leadership Principles," GeekWire, October 28, 2016, https://www.geekwire.com/2016/amazon-founder-jeff-bezos-offers-6-leadership-principles-change-mind-lot-embrace-failure-ditch-powerpoints/.

NOTES

45. For an overview of Amazon's failures, see Dennis Green, "Jeff Bezos Has Said That Amazon Has Had Failures Worth Billions of Dollars—Here Are Some of the Biggest Ones," *Business Insider*, July 5, 2019, https://www.businessinsider.com/amazon-products-services-failed-discontinued-2019-3.
46. Kirby and Stewart, "Institutional Yes."
47. Walmart is the largest.
48. Amazon, "Annual Reports, Proxies and Shareholder Letters," Amazon.com, accessed October 23, 2019, https://ir.aboutamazon.com/static-files/e01cc6e7-73df-4860-bd3d-95d366f29e57.
49. Stone, *Everything Store*, 90.
50. Kirby and Stewart, "Institutional Yes."
51. David Streitfeld and Christine Haughney, "Expecting the Unexpected from Jeff Bezos," *New York Times*, August 17, 2013, https://www.nytimes.com/2013/08/18/business/expecting-the-unexpected-from-jeff-bezos.html.
52. Day One Staff, "How Amazon Hires: The Story (and Song) Behind Amazon's Bar Raiser Program," The Amazon Blog, January 9, 2019, https://blog.aboutamazon.com/working-at-amazon/how-amazon-hires.
53. Alan Deutschman, "Inside the Mind of Jeff Bezos," *Fast Company*, August 1, 2004, https://www.fastcompany.com/50541/inside-mind-jeff-bezos-4.
54. Bezos, "2016 Letter to Shareholders."
55. Bezos, "2015 Letter to Shareholders."
56. Jeff Bezos, "2018 Letter to Shareholders," Amazon.com, April 11, 2019, https://ir.aboutamazon.com/static-files/4f64d0cd-12f2-4d6c-952e-bbed15ab1082.
57. Stone, *Everything Store*, 4.
58. Bezos, "2016 Letter to Shareholders."
59. Amazon installed air-conditioning soon after this incident, and has also done so in other fulfillment centers.
60. Bezos, "2018 Letter to Shareholders."
61. Bezos's difficult year included the decision to not establish a headquarters in New York City after a yearlong and highly publicized search. He failed to anticipate both the vocal opposition to the tax credits offered to Amazon and the perceived impact of housing availability in Long Island City by Amazon hiring an additional twenty-five thousand people. But the real surprise was that Amazon hadn't expected the political debate that emerged once it made its decision to establish a location in the city. See Eugene Kim, "Jeff Bezos Responds to Employee Concerns about His Personal Life: 'I Still Tap Dance into the Office,'" CNBC, March 11, 2019, https://www.cnbc.com/2019/03/11/bezos-responds-to-employee-concerns-about-his-personal-life.html.

Chapter Four: Building Great Products
1. Elon Musk, "Qualities of an Entrepreneur," Stanford University eCorner, October 8, 2003, https://ecorner.stanford.edu/video/qualities-of-an-entrepreneur/.
2. Angus MacKenzie, "2013 Motor Trend Car of the Year: Tesla Model S," *Car & Driver*, December 10, 2012, https://www.motortrend.com/news/2013-motor-trend-car-of-the-year-tesla-model-s/.

3. Consumer Reports rated the Model S P85D. See Mark Rechtin, "Tesla Model S P85D Earns Top Road Test Score," Consumer Reports, October 20, 2015, https://www.consumerreports.org/cro/cars/tesla-model-s-p85d-earns-top-road-test-score.

4. J. Clement, "Number of PayPal's Total Active Registered User Accounts from 1st Quarter 2010 to 2nd Quarter 2019 (in Millions)," Statista, July 26, 2019, https://www.statista.com/statistics/218493/paypals-total-active-registered-accounts-from-2010/.

5. Don Reisinger, "Elon Musk's Hyperloop Hit a New Top Speed of 288 MPH. But the Best Is Yet to Come," *Inc.*, July 22, 2019, https://www.inc.com/don-reisinger/elon-musks-hyperloop-hit-a-new-top-speed-of-288-mph-but-best-is-yet-to-come.html.

6. Elon Musk, "Founding of PayPal," Stanford University eCorner, October 8, 2003, https://ecorner.stanford.edu/video/founding-of-paypal/.

7. Brad Feld, "Great Entrepreneurs Are Obsessed with the Product," *Business Insider*, May 3, 2010, https://www.businessinsider.com/brad-feld-my-obsession-with-the-product-2010-5.

8. David Sheff, "Steve Jobs," *Playboy*, February 1, 1985, https://genius.com/David-sheff-playboy-interview-steve-jobs-annotated.

9. Isaacson, *Steve Jobs*, 570.

10. AutoTopNL, "Tesla Model S P90D 762 HP LUDRICOUS TOP SPEED & Acceleration on AUTOBAHN by AutoTopNL," YouTube video, March 22, 2016, https://www.youtube.com/watch?v=R1bG5nzjjdk.

11. Susan Pulliam, M. Ramsey, and Ianthe Dugan, "Elon Musk Sets Ambitious Goals at Tesla—and Often Falls Short," *Wall Street Journal*, August 15, 2016, https://www.wsj.com/articles/elon-musk-sets-ambitious-goals-at-teslaand-often-falls-short-1471275436.

12. Carol Hoffman, "Elon Musk, the Rocket Man with a Sweet Ride," *Smithsonian Magazine*, December 2012, https://www.smithsonianmag.com/science-nature/elon-musk-the-rocket-man-with-a-sweet-ride-136059680/.

13. Scott Pelley, "Tesla and SpaceX: Elon Musk's Industrial Empire," CBS *60 Minutes*, March 30, 2014, https://www.cbsnews.com/news/tesla-and-spacex-elon-musks-industrial-empire/.

14. Shobhit Seth, "How Much Can Facebook Potentially Make from Selling Your Data?," *Investopedia*, April 11, 2018, https://www.investopedia.com/tech/how-much-can-facebook-potentially-make-selling-your-data/.

15. LeBeau, Phil, "Tesla CEO Elon Musk's influence grows as automakers roll out electric-vehicle plans at Detroit auto show." CNBC. January 16, 2019, https://www.cnbc.com/2019/01/15/teslas-influence-grows-as-automakers-charge-up-electric-vehicle-plans.html.

16. Solmon Byike, "Elon Musk: We Are Running the Most Dangerous Experiment," Medium, August 3, 2017, https://medium.com/@SolomonByike/elon-musk-we-are-running-the-most-dangerous-experiment-e84eccee6044.

17. Elon Musk's Best Quotes on Business & Innovation," *Elon Musk News*, November 30, 2016,https://elonmusknews.org/blog/elon-musk-business-innovation-quotes.

18. Tommy.MS, "Elon Musk—Starting a Business," YouTube video, 3:09, August 31, 2014, https://www.youtube.com/watch?v=0Bo-RA0sGLU&feature=youtu.be.

19. Eric Loveday, "Elon Musk Gives Commencement Speech," InsideEVs, May 16, 2014, https://insideevs.com/elon-musk-gives-commencement-speech-video/.

20. Neil Strauss, "Elon Musk: The Architect of Tomorrow," *Rolling Stone*, November 15, 2017.

21. See Ken Kocienda's description of how Apple, and Steve Jobs in particular, viewed design in *Creative Selection* (New York: Saint Martin's Press, 2018), 187. Jobs described design as the soul of a product that is manifest at successive layers.

22. Neil Strauss, "Elon Musk: The Architect of Tomorrow," *Rolling Stone*, November 15, 2017.

23. Robin Keats, "Rocket Man," *Queen's Alumni Review*, no. 3 (2019), https://www.queensu.ca/gazette/alumnireview/stories/rocket-man.

24. Ashlee Vance, *Elon Musk: Tesla, SpaceX, and the Quest for a Fantastic Future* (New York: Harper Collins, 2015), 230.

25. Richard Feloni, "Former SpaceX Exec Explains How Elon Musk Taught Himself Rocket Science," *Business Insider*, October 23, 2014, https://www.businessinsider.com/how-elon-musk-learned-rocket-science-for-spacex-2014-10; Tom Junod, "Elon Musk: Triumph of His Will," *Esquire*, November 15, 2012, https://www.esquire.com/news-politics/a16681/elon-musk-interview-1212/.

26. Mike Ramsey, "Electric-Car Pioneer Elon Musk Charges Head-On at Detroit," *Wall Street Journal*, January 11, 2015, https://www.wsj.com/articles/electric-car-pioneer-elon-musk-charges-head-on-at-detroit-1421033527.

27. Elon Musk, interview with Barry Hurd for The Henry Ford, SpaceX, Hawthorne, California, June 26, 2008, https://www.thehenryford.org/docs/default-source/default-document-library/default-document-library/transcript_musk_full-length.pdf.

28. Logan Ward, "Elon Musk Will Save the Planet—And Then Leave It Behind," *Popular Mechanics*, October 1, 2012, https://www.popularmechanics.com/technology/a8217/elon-musk-will-save-the-planet-and-then-leave-it-behind-13210592/.

29. Chris Anderson, "The Shared Genius of Elon Musk and Steve Jobs," *Fortune*, November 21, 2013, https://fortune.com/2013/11/21/the-shared-genius-of-elon-musk-and-steve-jobs/.

30. "5 Steps to Becoming Extraordinary," *Sri Lanka Sunday Times*, July 8, 2018, https://www.pressreader.com/sri-lanka/sunday-times-sri-lanka/20180708/283257393633306.

31. Loveday, "Elon Musk Gives Commencement Speech."

32. Meghan Daum, "Elon Musk Wants to Change How (and Where) Humans Live," *Vogue*, September 21, 2015, https://www.vogue.com/article/elon-musk-profile-entrepreneur-spacex-tesla-motors.

33. Bloomberg, "Elon Musk: How I Became the Real 'Iron Man,'" YouTube video, 44:59, January 10, 2014, https://www.youtube.com/watch?v=mh45igK4Esw&feature=youtu.be.

34. Vance, *Elon Musk*, 48.

35. Lee, "Secrets to Elon Musk's Success."

36. Jade Scipioni, "Why Bill Gates Says His 20-Year-Old Self Would Be 'So Disgusted' with Him Today," CNBC, June 25, 2019, https://www.cnbc.com/2019/06/25/why-bill-gates-younger-self-would-be-disgusted-with-him-today.html.

37. Auto Bild, "Tesla CEO Elon Musk," YouTube video, 34:01, November 5, 2014, https://www.youtube.com/watch?v=FE4iFYqi4QU.

38. Chris Anderson, "Elon Musk's Mission to Mars," *Wired*, October 21, 2012, https://www.wired.com/2012/10/ff-elon-musk-qa/.

39. O'Reilley, "Conversation with Elon Musk (Tesla Motors)—Web 2.0 Summit 08," YouTube video, 29:35, November 10, 2008, https://www.youtube.com/watch?v=gVwmNaPsxLc.

40. Kamelia Angelova, "How Elon Musk Can Tell If Job Applicants Are Lying About Their Experience," *Business Insider*, December 26, 2013, https://www.businessinsider.com.au/elon-musk-rule-job-interviews-lying-tesla-2015-6.

41. Glassdoor, April 8, 2014, https://www.glassdoor.com/Interview/fremont-tesla-motors-interview-questions-SRCH_IL.0,7_IC1147355_KE8,20.htm.

42. Sebastian Blanco, "In Deep with Tesla CEO Elon Musk: Financials, Falcon Doors and Finding Faults in the Model S," Autoblog, September 7, 2012, https://www.autoblog.com/2012/09/07/tesla-ceo-elon-musk-q-and-a/.

43. CHM Revolutionaries: An Evening with Elon Musk. February 5, 2013. https://www.youtube.com/watch?v=AHHwXUm3iIg.

44. David Gelles et al., "Elon Musk Details 'Excruciating' Personal Toll of Tesla Turmoil," *New York Times*, August 16, 2018, https://www.nytimes.com/2018/08/16/business/elon-musk-interview-tesla.html.

45. Sal Khan, "Elon Musk—CEO of Tesla Motors and SpaceX," Khan Academy, April 17, 2013, https://www.khanacademy.org/college-careers-more/entrepreneurship2/interviews-entrepreneurs/copy-of-khan-academy-living-room-chats/v/elon-musk.

46. Ian Bogost, "Elon Musk Is His Own Worst Enemy," *Atlantic*, September 28, 2018, https://www.theatlantic.com/technology/archive/2018/09/sec-might-push-elon-musk-out-tesla/571606/.

47. Tae Kim, "Former Big Bull on Tesla Says the Stock Is 'No Longer Investable' Due to Elon Musk's Behavior," CNBC, September 11, 2018, https://www.cnbc.com/2018/09/11/former-big-bull-on-tesla-says-the-stock-is-no-longer-investable-due-to-elon-musks-behavior.html.

48. Thomas Barrabi, "Tesla Is 'No Longer Investable' Due to Elon Musk's Antics, Firm Says," Fox Business, September 11, 2018, https://www.foxbusiness.com/business-leaders/tesla-is-no-longer-investable-due-to-elon-musks-antics-firm-says.

49. Berkely Lovelace Jr., "Cramer on Musk Pot Stunt: This Is 'Behavior of a Man Who Should Not Be Running a Public Company,'" https://www.cnbc.com/2018/09/07/cramer-on-weed-stunt-musk-should-not-be-running-a-public-company.html.

50. Anderson, "Elon Musk's Mission to Mars."

51. Apple now faces the opposite problem as Musk in finding a product visionary to replace Steve Jobs along with the recently resigned chief design officer Jony Ive. While Tim Cook is respected for his management of Apple, most don't see him

as being that person. In 2019, Apple introduced a credit card that it touted as being titanium, laser-etched, and with no card number—which suggest Apple is a company no longer intent on "putting a dent in the universe."

52. Vance, *Elon Musk*, 222.
53. Vance, 73–74.
54. Vance, 73–74.
55. Shane Snow, "Steve Jobs's and Elon Musk's Counterintuitive Leadership Traits," *Fast Company*, June 4, 2015, https://www.fastcompany.com/3046916/elon-musks -leadership-traits.
56. Vance, *Elon Musk*, 362.
57. Melody Hahm, "Timeline: The Mass Exodus of Tesla Execs in the Last 12 Months," Yahoo Finance, February 20, 2019, https://finance.yahoo.com/news /tesla-layoffs-execs-leaving-133852528.html.
58. Vance, *Elon Musk*, 176.
59. Elon Musk, "The Henry Ford Visionaries of Innovation," The Henry Ford, 2008, https://www.thehenryford.org/explore/stories-of-innovation/visionaries/elon-musk/.

Chapter Five : Juicing Growth

1. Mike Isaac, "Uber's C.E.O. Plays with Fire," *New York Times*, April 23, 2017, https://www.nytimes.com/2017/04/23/technology/travis-kalanick-pushes-uber -and-himself-to-the-precipice.html.
2. Adam Lashinsky, *Wild Ride: Inside Uber's Quest for World Domination* (New York: Penguin, 2017), 41.
3. Alyson Shontell, "All Hail the Uber Man! How Sharp-Elbowed Salesman Travis Kalanick Became Silicon Valley's Newest Star Business," *Insider*, January 11, 2014, https://www.businessinsider.com/uber-travis-kalanick -bio-2014-1.
4. Max Chafkin, "What Makes Uber Run," *Fast Company*, September 18, 2015, https://www.fastcompany.com/3050250/what-makes-uber-run.
5. Chafkin, "What Makes Uber Run."
6. One source indicates that Akamai acquired RedSwoosh for $23 million, with $19 million in stock and $4 million in earn-outs. See Alyson Shontell, "All Hail The Uber Man! How Sharp-Elbowed Salesman Travis Kalanick Became Silicon Valley's Newest Star," *Business Insider*, January 14, 2014, https://www.businessinsider.com /uber-travis-kalanick-bio-2014-1.
7. Mike Isaac, "Uber's C.E.O. Plays with Fire," *New York Times*, April 23, 2017, https://www.nytimes.com/2017/04/23/technology/travis-kalanick-pushes-uber -and-himself-to-the-precipice.html.
8. Lashinsky, *Wild Ride*, 71–72.
9. Kara Swisher, "Man and Uber Man," *Vanity Fair*, November 5, 2014, https://archive.vanityfair.com/article/2018/11/man-and-uber-man.
10. Nick Bilton, "Why Uber Might Have to Fire Travis Kalanick," *Vanity Fair*, June 16, 2017, https://www.vanityfair.com/news/2017/06/why-uber-might-have-to -fire-travis-kalanick.

11. Sergei Klebnikov, "Uber Could be Worth $100 Billion After Its IPO: Here's Who Stands to Make the Most Money," *Money*, April 12, 2019, http://money.com /money/5641631/uber-ipo-billionaires/.

12. Yahoo, "How a Trip to Zimbabwe Became the Inspiration for Lyft," YouTube video, March 31, 2016, https://www.youtube.com/watch?v=dk1URUz198U.

13. Lora Kolodny, "Uber Prices IPO at $45 Per Share, Toward the Low End of the Range," CNBC, May 9, 2019, https://www.cnbc.com/2019/05/09/uber-ipo -pricing.html.

14. Uber, "Company Info," Uber Newsroom, accessed October 23, 2019, https://www.uber.com/newsroom/company-info/.

15. Rana Foroohar, "Person of the Year: The Short List #6—Travis Kalanick," *Time*, December 7, 2015, https://time.com/time-person-of-the-year-2015-runner-up -travis-kalanick/.

16. Olivia Vanni, "Here's What Uber's CEO Told MIT Students about Entrepreneurship," BOSTINNO, December 3, 2015, https://www.americaninno .com/boston/uber-ceo-kalanick-entrepreneur-and-startup-advice/.

17. TechCrunch, "Disrupt Backstage: Travis Kalanick," YouTube video, 8:41, June 22, 2011, https://www.youtube.com/watch?v=0-uiO-P9yEg.

18. Olivia Nuzzi, "Uber Hires Ex-Obama Campaign Manager to Help Fight 'Big Taxi Cartel,'" *Daily Beast*, April 14, 2017, https://www.thedailybeast.com /uber-hires-ex-obama-campaign-manager-to-help-fight-big-taxi-cartel.

19. Evan Carmichael, "Travis Kalanick's Top 10 Rules For Success (@travisk)," YouTube video, 18:03, October 26, 2016, https://www.youtube.com /watch?v=2Ih9mug8m2g.

20. Prior to becoming Uber's CEO, "Kalanick started investing small amounts of money in various startups with the understanding that he'd be available as their own personal fixer, willing to swoop in and solve problems whenever a founder needed his help." Shweta Modgil, "Fall in Love with an Idea and Just Go After It: Travis Kalanick, CEO Uber," Inc42, January 21, 2016, https://inc42.com/buzz /travis-kalanick-ceo-uber/ 1/21/2016.

21. Graham Rapier, "Uber's Ousted Founder Travus Kalanik Would Like You to Call Him 'T-bone,'" *Business Insider*, September 3, 2019, https://www.businessinsider .my/uber-founder-travis-kalanick-used-t-bone-nickname-2019-9/.

22. Oliver Stanley, Uber Has Replaced Travis Kalanick's Values with Eight New 'Cultural Norms,'" *Quartz*, November 7, 2017, https://qz.com/work/1123038 /uber-has-replaced-travis-kalanicks-values-with-eight-new-cultural-norms/.

23. Swisher, "Man and Uber Man."

24. Bilton, "Why Uber Might Have to Fire Travis Kalanick."

25. Max Chafkin, "What Makes Uber Run," *Fast Company*, September 8, 2015, https://www.fastcompany.com/3050250/what-makes-uber-run.

26. Foroohar, "Travis Kalanick."

27. Swisher, "Man and Uber Man."

28. Sean Stanton, a former colleague of Kalanick, noted, "Scour was about efficiency. Swoosh was about efficiency. It's just the way his brain is wired. It's like the way

Uber works right now: What's the fastest, cheapest and most efficient way to get from point A to point B? That consumes him, and all parts of his life." Isaac, "Uber's C.E.O. Plays with Fire."

29. Olivia Nuzzi, "Inside Uber's Political War Machine," *Daily Beast*, June 30, 2014, https://www.thedailybeast.com/inside-ubers-political-war-machine.

30. At the time, Uber was dealing with widespread account fraud in China, where some drivers bought stolen iPhones that were erased and resold. These drivers would then create dozens of fake email addresses and sign up for new Uber rider accounts. They would request rides from the phones, which they would then accept. Since Uber was paying incentives to drivers to take more rides, the drivers could unethically earn more money. See Isaac, "Uber's CEO Plays with Fire."

31. Mike Isaac, Katie Benner, and Sheera Frenkel, "Uber Hid 2016 Break, Paying Hackers to Delete Stolen Data," *New York Times*, November 21, 2017, https://www.nytimes.com/2017/11/21/technology/uber-hack.html.

32. Ian Wren, "Uber, Google's Waymo Settle Case Over Trade Secrets for Self-Driving Cars," NPR, February 9, 2018, https://www.npr.org/sections/thetwo-way/2018/02/09/584522541/uber-googles-waymo-settle-case-over-trade-secrets-for-self-driving-cars. The legal damages were paid with 0.34 percent of Uber's stock.

33. David Z. Morris, "Uber's Self-Driving Systems, Not Human Drivers, Missed at Least Six Red Lights in San Francisco," *Fortune*, February 26, 2017, https://fortune.com/2017/02/26/uber-self-driving-car-red-lights/.

34. Susan Fowler, "Reflecting on One Very, Very Strange Year at Uber," Susan Fowler (blog), February 19, 2017, https://www.susanjfowler.com/blog/2017/2/19/reflecting-on-one-very-strange-year-at-uber. Fowler writes, "My new manager sent me a string of messages over company chat. He was in an open relationship, he said, and his girlfriend was having an easy time finding new partners but he wasn't. He was trying to stay out of trouble at work, he said, but he couldn't help getting in trouble, because he was looking for women to have sex with. It was clear that he was trying to get me to have sex with him, and it was so clearly out of line that I immediately took screenshots of these chat messages and reported him to HR."

35. Maya Kosoff, "Don't Cry for Travis Kalanick," *Vanity Fair*, June 21, 2017, https://www.vanityfair.com/news/2017/06/dont-cry-for-travis-kalanick.

36. Kurt Bowermaster, "Uber Driving in Central Iowa," Facebook, June 4, 2015, https://www.facebook.com/UberKurt/posts/here-are-uber-ceo-travis-kalanicks-remarks-from-ubers-five-year-anniversary-cele/516756488472094/.

37. The shareholder letter was titled "Moving Uber Forward." See Ainslee Harris's article "Uber's Ousted CEO Travis Kalanick Discovered the Limits of Founder Control—The Hard Way," *Fast Company*, June 21, 2017, https://www.fastcompany.com/40433780/uber-ceo-travis-kalanick-learns-the-hard-way-that-founder-control-has-limits.

38. Anita Balakrishnan, "Uber Investor Bill Gurley: My Firm was 'On the Right Side of History' for Ousting Travis Kalanick," Yahoo Finance, November 17, 2017, https://finance.yahoo.com/news/uber-investor-bill-gurley-firm-171146265.html.

39. Mike Isaac, "Uber Founder Travis Kalanick Resigns as C.E.O.," *New York Times*, June 21, 2017, https://www.nytimes.com/2017/06/21/technology/uber-ceo-travis-kalanick.html.

40. Maya Kosoff, "Uber's New C.E.O. Says Travis Kalanick was 'Guilty of Hubris,'" *Vanity Fair*, January 23, 2018, https://www.vanityfair.com/news/2018/01/ubers-new-ceo-says-travis-kalanick-was-guilty-of-hubris.

41. For two very different views of Steve Jobs's influence on Pixar, see: Alvy Ray Smith, "Pixar History Revisited—A Corrective," Pixar Animation Studios, accessed October 23, 2019, http://alvyray.com/Pixar/PixarHistoryRevisited.htm, and Robert Iger, "'We Could Say Anything to Each Other': Bob Iger Remembers Steve Jobs, the Pixar Drama, and the Apple Merger That Wasn't," *Vanity Fair*, September 18, 2019, https://www.vanityfair.com/news/2019/09/bob-iger-remembers-steve-jobs#.

42. Alison Griswold, "There Would Be No Uber Without Travis Kalanick," *Quartz*, June 22, 2017, https://qz.com/1011300/uber-ceo-travis-kalanick-pissed-people-off-and-it-made-the-company-great/.

43. Kosoff, "Uber's New C.E.O."

44. Mike Isaac and Katie Benner, "'Nobody Is Perfect': Some Uber Employees Balk at Travis Kalanick's Exit," *New York Times*, June 22, 2017, https://www.nytimes.com/2017/06/22/technology/uber-employees-react-travis-kalanick.html.

45. Tiku Nitasha, "Travis Kalanick and the Last Gasp of Tech's Alpha CEOs," *Wired*, June 21, 2017, https://www.wired.com/story/travis-kalanick-uber-ceo-leave/.

46. Thomas Lee, "Marissa Mayer Defends Former Uber CEO Travis Kalanick," *San Francisco Chronicle*, June 27, 2017, https://www.sfchronicle.com/business/article/Marissa-Mayer-defends-former-Uber-CEO-Travis-11251256.php.

47. Lashinsky, *Wild Ride*.

48. Kara Swisher and Johana Bhuiyan, "Uber CEO Kalanick Advised Employees on Sex Rules for a Company Celebration in 2013 'Miami letter,'" *Vox*, June 8, 2017, https://www.vox.com/2017/6/8/15765514/2013-miami-letter-uber-ceo-kalanick-employees-sex-rules-company-celebration.

49. Peter Thiel stated that "Uber is the most ethically challenged company in Silicon Valley." Thiel is an investor in Lyft, Uber's primary competitor in the US. See Laurie Segall, "Peter Thiel: Uber Is 'Most Ethically Challenged Company in Silicon Valley,'" CNN Business, November 18, 2014, https://money.cnn.com/2014/11/18/technology/uber-unethical-peter-thiel/.

50. Nitasha, "Travis Kalanick and the Last Gasp of Tech's Alpha CEOs."

51. Kara Swisher and Johana Bhuiyan, "Uber President Jeff Jones Is Quitting, Citing Differences Over 'Beliefs and Approach to Leadership,'" *Vox*, March 19, 2017, https://www.vox.com/2017/3/19/14976110/uber-president-jeff-jones-quits.

52. Marcus Wholsen, "What Uber Will Do with All That Money from Google," *Wired*, January 3, 2014, https://www.wired.com/2014/01/uber-travis-kalanick/.

53. Shontell, "All Hail the Uber Man!"

54. Nitasha, "Travis Kalanick and the Last Gasp of Tech's Alpha CEOs."

55. Rachel Holt, Andrew Macdonald, and Pierre-Dimitri Gore-Coty, "5 Billion Trips," Uber Newsroom, June 29, 2017, https://www.uber.com/newsroom/5billion-2/.

56. Jake Novak, "The Hunting Down of Uber's Travis Kalanick," CNBC, June 24, 2017, https://www.cnbc.com/2017/06/23/the-poaching-of-travis-kalanick.html. Novak argues that those who challenge the status quo in entrenched industries (taxi, automotive) face attacks by those threatened by the threat they pose.

57. Johana Bhuiyan, "Uber CEO Travis Kalanick Admits He 'Must Fundamentally Change as a Leader and Grow Up,'" *Vox*, February 28, 2017, https://www.vox.com/2017/2/28/14772416/uber-ceo-travis-kalanick-apology-driver.

58. Timothy Lee, "The Latest Uber Scandal, Explained," *Vox*, November 19, 2014, https://www.vox.com/2014/11/19/7248819/uber-scandal-explained.

59. Jacob Kastrenakes, "Uber Executive Casually Threatens Journalist with Smear Campaign," Verge, November 18, 2014, https://www.theverge.com/2014/11/18/7240215/uber-exec-casually-threatens-sarah-lacy-with-smear-campaign.

60. John Gapper, "Travis Kalanick Is Not Ethical Enough to Steer Uber," *Financial Times*, June 13, 2017, https://www.ft.com/content/7a1b6f24-502f-11e7-bfb8-997009366969.

61. Stone, *Everything Store*, 318.

62. Charles Duhigg, "Is Amazon Unstoppable?" *New Yorker*, October 10, 2019, https://www.newyorker.com/magazine/2019/10/21/is-amazon-unstoppable.

63. For more on the three-factor model of trust and its impact, see my book *Trust in the Balance* (San Francisco: Jossey-Bass, 1997). For an analysis of trust research over several decades, see Donald L. Ferrin and Kurt T. Dirks, "Trust in Leadership: Meta-Analytic Findings and Implications for Research and Practice," *Journal of Applied Psychology* 87, no. 4 (2002): 611–28.

64. Chafkin, "What Makes Uber Run"; Swisher, "Man and Uber Man."

65. John Gapper, "Travis Kalanick Lacks the Ethics to Steer Uber," *Financial Review Times*, June 15, 2017, https://www.ft.com/content/7a1b6f24-502f-11e7-bfb8-997009366969.

66. Facebook is a visible example of a founder retaining control. Mark Zuckerberg holds 57 percent of Facebook's voting stock, which gives him control (regardless of what the firm's board or shareholders might want). He structured the firm to ensure his control—which, depending on one's point of view about the role of powerful leaders, is positive (in allowing the founder to manage for the long term) and/or negative (in failing to have necessary checks and balances).

67. Noam Wasserman, "The Founder's Dilemma," *Harvard Business Review*, February 2008, https://hbr.org/2008/02/the-founders-dilemma.

68. Ari Levy, "When $8 Billion Is Yours to Lose: How Uber's Top Investor Suffered Through the Wildest Tech Drama of the Year," CNBC, December 15, 2017, https://www.cnbc.com/2017/12/14/bill-gurley-2017-profile-uber-stitchfix-snap.html.

69. Kosoff, "Don't Cry for Travis Kalanick."

Chapter Six: The Individual's Choice

1. Peter Drucker, *Adventures of a Bystander* (New Brunswick: Transaction Publishers, 2009), 255. Stuart Bunderson and Jeffery A. Thompson, "The Call of the Wild: Zookeepers, Callings, and the Double-Edged Sword of Deeply Meaningful

Work," *Administrative Science Quarterly* 54, no. 1 (March 2009), https://journals
.sagepub.com/doi/10.2189/asqu.2009.54.1.32.

2. Bunderson and Thompson, "Call of the Wild."

3. Bunderson and Thompson, "Call of the Wild."

4. Bunderson and Thompson, "Call of the Wild."

5. J. Y. Kim et al., "Understanding Contemporary Form of Exploitation: Attributions of
    Passion Serve to Legitimize the Poor Treatment of Workers," *Journal of Personality and
    Social Psychology*, April 18, 2019, http://dx.doi.org/10.1037/pspi0000190.

6. "Vocation," Merriam Webster Dictionary, https://www.merriam-webster.com
    /dictionary/vocation.

7. Paul W. Robinson (ed.), *The Annotated Luther, Volume 3: Church and Sacraments*
    (Minneapolis: Free Press, 1989), 81.

8. Ruth Umoh, "Jeff Bezos: You Can Have a Job or a Career, But if You Have
    This You've 'Hit the Jackpot,'" CNBC, May 7, 2018, https://www.cnbc
    .com/2018/05/07/jeff-bezos-gives-this-career-advice-to-young-employees.html.

9. Hanson Hosein, "Four Peaks: My Interview with Jeff Bezos," YouTube video,
    22:36, September 13, 2013, https://www.youtube.com/watch?v=vhDRBPCOxmA.

10. Marc Myers, "For Mark Knopfler, a Red Guitar Started It All," *Wall Street
    Journal*, May 21, 2019, https://www.wsj.com/articles/for-mark-knopfler-a-red
    -guitar-started-it-all-11558445862.

11. P. A. O'Keefe, C. S. Dweck, and G. M. Walton, "Implicit Theories of Interest:
    Finding Your Passion or Developing It?," *Psychological Science,* September 6, 2018,
    https://journals.sagepub.com/doi/abs/10.1177/0956797618780643.

12. Jessica Stillman, "Which Comes First, Work or Passion?," *Inc.*, October 12, 2012,
    https://www.inc.com/jessica-stillman/hard-work-or-passion.html.

13. Melissa Witte, "Instead of 'Finding Your Passion,' Try Developing It, Stanford
    Scholars Say," Stanford News, June 18, 2018, https://news.stanford.edu/press
    -releases/2018/06/18/find-passion-may-bad-advice/.

14. Jonathan Shieber, "How Airbnb Went from Renting Air Beds for $10 to a $30
    Billion Hospitality Behemoth," TechCrunch, August 12, 2018,
    https://techcrunch.com/2018/08/12/how-airbnb-went-from-renting-air-beds-for
    -10-to-a-30-billion-hospitality-behemoth/.

15. Airbnb Newsroom, "Fast Facts," Airbnb, https://press.airbnb.com/fast-facts/.

16. O'Keefe, Dweck, and Walton, "Implicit Theories of Interest."

17. Attributed to Noel Coward.

18. Steve Jobs, "'You've Got to Find What You Love,' Jobs Says," Stanford News, June
    14, 2005, https://news.stanford.edu/2005/06/14/jobs-061505/.

19. Karl Ericsson, Clemens Tesch-Roemer, and Ralf T. Krampe, "The Role of
    Deliberate Practice in the Acquisition of Expert Performance," *Psychological
    Review* 100, no. 3 (July 1993): 363–406.

20. Mark Leibovich, *The New Imperialists* (New York: Prentice Hall Press,
    2002), 78.

21. CNBC, "Jeff Bezos at the Economic Club of Washington," YouTube video,
    1:09:57, September 13, 2018, https://www.youtube.com/watch?v=xv_vkA0jsyo.

22. Caroline Adams and Michael B. Frisch, *Creating Your Best Life: The Ultimate Life List Guide* (New York: Sterling, 2009), 144.

23. Adams and Frisch, 144.

24. Newport, *So Good They Can't Ignore You*, 39.

25. Charles Duhigg, "Wealthy, Successful and Miserable," *New York Magazine*, February 21, 2019, https://www.nytimes.com/interactive/2019/02/21/magazine /elite-professionals-jobs-happiness.html.

26. See Newport, *So Good They Can't Ignore You*.

27. For a humorous portrayal of the eternal reoccurrence, see the movie *Groundhog Day*, directed by Harold Ramis (Culver City, CA: Columbia Pictures, 1993).

28. Fredrich Nietzsche, *The Gay Science* (New York: Vintage Books, 1974), 273.

29. Mihaly Csikszentmihalyi, *Flow: The Psychology of Optimal Experience* (New York: Harper Perennial Modern Classics, 2008).

30. Micky Thompson, "Jeff Bezos - Regret Minimization Framework," YouTube video, December 20, 2008, https://www.youtube.com/watch?v=jwG _qR6XmDQ.

31. Jobs, "You've Got to Find What You Love."

32. Susan Orlean, *The Orchid Thief: A True Story of Beauty and Obsession* (New York: Random House, 1998), 132.

33. Orlean, *Orchard Thief*, 336.

34. Gary Burnison, "Breaking Boredom: What's Really Driving Job Seekers in 2018," Korn Ferry Institute, January 8, 2018, https://www.kornferry.com/institute/job -hunting-2018-boredom.

35. Marcus Fairs, "Silicon Valley 'Didn't Think a Designer Could Build a Company,' Says Airbnb Co-Founder Brian Chesky," *Dezeen*, January 28, 2014, https://www .dezeen.com/2014/01/28/silicon-valley-didnt-think-a-designer-could-build-a -company-interview-airbnb-co-founder-brian-chesky/.

36. David Foster Wallace, "String Theory," *Esquire*, July 1996, https://www.esquire .com/sports/a5151/the-string-theory-david-foster-wallace/.

37. SpaceX, "SpaceX Launch—SpaceX Employees Cheering Outside Mission Control," YouTube, 0:28, May 22, 2012, https://www.youtube.com/watch?v=6XtD-5L7cLk.

38. David Sheff, "Playboy Interview: Steve Jobs," *Playboy*, February 1985, http://reprints.longform.org/playboy-interview-steve-jobs.

39. Derek Thompson, "Workism Is Making Americans Miserable," *Atlantic*, February 24, 2019, https://www.theatlantic.com/ideas/archive/2019/02/religion-workism -making-americans-miserable/583441/.

40. Chad Day, "Americans Have Shifted Dramatically on What Matters Most," *Wall Street Journal*, August 25, 2019, https://www.wsj.com/articles/americans-have -shifted-dramatically-on-what-values-matter-most-11566738001. The poll found that hard work tops the list across all age groups, while belief in religion is much lower among those in the 18–38 age cohort.

41. Karen Gilchrist, "Alibaba Founder Jack Ma Says Working Overtime Is a 'Huge Blessing,'" CNBC, April 15, 2019, https://www.cnbc.com/2019/04/15/alibabas -jack-ma-working-overtime-is-a-huge-blessing.html.

42. Erin Griffith, "Why Are Young People Pretending to Love Work?," *New York Times*, January 26, 2019, https://www.nytimes.com/2019/01/26/business/against -hustle-culture-rise-and-grind-tgim.html.

43. Griffith.

44. Ryan Avent, "Is Your Obsession with Working Hard Just Professional Stockholm Syndrome," *Financial Review*, April 2, 2016, https://www.afr.com/life-and -luxury/arts-and-culture/why-do-we-work-so-hard-do-we-have-professional -stockholm-syndrome-20160328-gnsgmg.

45. Thompson, "Workism Is Making Americans Miserable."

46. Thompson.

47. The idea of what one is willing to sacrifice to achieve vocational mastery and power is captured fictionally in the legend of Faust. In different versions, Faust is portrayed as having sold his soul to the devil in return for being granted extraordinary talents. A version of the Faust legend is the story of Robert Johnson, the legendary American blues musician.

48. *Steve Jobs: The Man in the Machine*, directed by Alex Gibney (New York: Magnolia Pictures, 2015).

49. Alan Shipnuck, "Kevin Na Is Fit to be Tied (Just Ask Him)," *Sports Illustrated*, January 18, 2016, https://www.si.com/vault/2016/02/11/kevin-na-fit-be-tied-just -ask-him.

50. Lane Florsheim, "Annie Leibovitz on Being Envious of Herself," *Wall Street Journal*, February 13, 2019, https://www.wsj.com/articles/annie-leibovitz-on -being-envious-of-herself-11550088650.

51. Jena McGregor, "Elon Musk Is the 'Poster Boy' of a Culture That Celebrates 'Obsessive Overwork,'" *The Washington Post*, August 23, 2018, https://www .washingtonpost.com/business/2018/08/22/elon-musk-is-poster-boy-culture -that-celebrates-obsessive-overwork/.

52. Josh Constine, "Jeff Bezos' Guide to Life," TechCrunch, November 5, 2017, https://techcrunch.com/2017/11/05/jeff-bezos-guide-to-life/.

53. Mathias Dopfner, "Jeff Bezos Reveals What It's Like to Build an Empire and Become the Richest Man in the World—and Why He's Willing to Spend $1 Billion a Year to Fund the Most Important Mission of His Life," *Business Insider*, April 28, 2018, https://www.businessinsider.com/jeff-bezos-interview -axel-springer-ceo-amazon-trump-blue-origin-family-regulation-washington -post-2018-4.

54. "First Among Men," *Sydney Morning Herald*, February 14, 2015, https://www .smh.com.au/world/first-among-men-20140210-32amz.html. Lagarde said that she wished her male colleagues would experience a bit more guilt for family sacrifices but was not sure they do.

55. Adam Lashinsky, "Riding Shotgun with Uber CEO Travis Kalanick," *Fortune*, May 18, 2017, https://fortune.com/2017/05/18/uber-travis-kalanick-wild-ride/.

56. Scott Carrell, M. Hoekstra, and J. West, "Is Poor Fitness Contagious? Evidence from Randomly Assigned Friends," *Journal of Public Economics* 95, no. 7–8 (August 2011): 657–63, https://ideas.repec.org/a/eee/pubeco/v95y2011i7-8p657-663.html.

57. Research also indicates that a high-performing leader can positively influence team members by setting a high standard and modeling the "right" behaviors. For details on how this occurs, see Sam Walker's *The Captain Class* (London: Random House, 2017). The Air Force study demonstrates that peers are also important in determining how well a team and its members function.

58. Elizabeth Campbell et al., "Hot Shots and Cool Reception: An Expanded View of Social Consequences for High Performers," *Journal of Applied Psychology* 102, no. 5 (2017): 845–66, https://www.researchgate.net/publication/313686960 _Hot_Shots_and_Cool_Reception_An_Expanded_View_of_Social _Consequences_for_High_Performers.

59. The researchers also found that highly collaborative environments resulted in less support and more mistreatment of high performers. They suggest this occurs because a team-based company or group strives to create a common and collaborative environment where no one stands alone or, in this case, above the team.

60. The researchers showed that zookeepers with a sense of calling were more willing to sacrifice money, time, and physical comfort for their work.

61. Jim Edwards, "Reddit's Alexis Ohanian Says 'Hustle Porn' Is 'One of the Most Toxic, Dangerous Things in Tech Right Now,'" *Business Insider*, November 6, 2018, https://www.businessinsider.com/reddit-alexis-ohanian-hustle-porn-toxic -dangerous-thing-in-tech-2018-11.

62. Brad Stulberg and S. Magness, *Peak Performance: Elevate Your Game, Avoid Burnout and Thrive with the New Science* (Emmaus, PA: Rodale Press, 2017), loc. 393 of 3613. Kindle.

63. Robert J. Vallerand, *The Psychology of Passion: A Dualistic Model* (Oxford: Oxford University Press, 2015).

64. Vallerand developed a sixteen-item questionnaire that assesses what he proposes are two types of passion. Six of the questions identify obsession passion and six identify harmonious passion. See the Passion Toward Work Scale (PTWS) in Vallerand, *Psychology of Passion*.

65. "Jeff Bezos," The Economic Club of Washington, DC.

66. Arianna Huffington, "An Open Letter to Elon Musk," Thrive Global, August 17, 2018, https://thriveglobal.com/stories/open-letter-elon-musk/.

67. See my book *Leadership Blindspots* (San Francisco: Jossey Bass, 2014) for more on how blind spots operate and the actions that individuals and organizations can take to manage them effectively.

Chapter Seven: The Organization's Challenge

1. In German, *Vergeltungswaffe Zwei*. Its name was in response to the Allied bombing of German cities.

2. John Noble Wilford, "Wernher von Braun, Rocket Pioneer, Dies," *New York Times*, June 18, 1977.

3. Alejandro de la Garza, "How Historians Are Reckoning with the Former Nazi Who Launched America's Space Program," *TIME*, July 18, 2019, https://time .com/5627637/nasa-nazi-von-braun/.

4. Michael Neufeld, *Von Braun: Dreamer of Space, Engineer of War* (New York: Vintage Books, 2007), 5. Some argue that Sergei Korolev played an even more important role in leading Russia's space efforts.

5. "Biography of Wernher Von Braun," NASA, accessed October 23, 2019, https://www.nasa.gov/centers/marshall/history/vonbraun/bio.html.

6. Neufeld, *Von Braun*, 351.

7. Michael J. Neufeld, "Wernher von Baun, the SS, and Concentration Camp Labor: Questions of Moral, Political, and Criminal Responsibility," *German Studies Review* 25, no. 1 (February 2002): 57–78.

8. A similar case is that of German engineer Ferdinand Porche. He founded VW and designed what became the Beetle with Hitler's enthusiastic support. Porche also contributed to the design and manufacturing of German military equipment, including all-terrain vehicles and tanks. Like von Braun, he was a member of the Nazi party and SS, and his manufacturing plants used slave labor. Porche was jailed in France for war crimes in 1945 but released after his family paid a bail to the French government. He was never convicted of war crimes and died in 1951.

9. Wilford, "Wernher von Braun."

10. Pat Harrison, "American Might: Where 'The Good and the Bad Are All Mixed Up,'" *Radcliffe Magazine*, https://www.radcliffe.harvard.edu/news/radcliffe -magazine/american-might-where-good-and-bad-are-all-mixed. The quote is from folk singer Pete Seeger, upon hearing of Diane McWhorter's book on the history of von Braun and the Marshall Space Center.

11. There is also debate regarding von Braun's moral responsibility for building weapons capable of killing people on a mass scale. Von Braun justified how the US treated him after the war. He said that if Germany had won the war, "We wouldn't have treated your atomic scientists as war criminals, and I didn't expect to be treated as one. . . . The V2 was something we had and you didn't have. Naturally, you wanted to know all about it." Wilford, "Wernher von Braun."

12. Brian E. Crim, *Our Germans: Project Paperclip and the National Security State* (Baltimore, John Hopkins University Press, 2018), 192.

13. Neufled describes von Braun as a twentieth-century Faust—a man who sold his soul in exchange for gifts that allowed him to achieve his dream.

14. US Securities and Exchange Commission, "Elon Musk Settles SEC Fraud Charges; Tesla Charged with and Resolves Securities Law Charge," SEC.gov, September 29, 2018, https://www.sec.gov/news/press-release/2018-226.

15. Kevin LaCroix, "Tesla Investors File Securities Suits Over Elon Musk's Take -Private Tweets," D&O Diary, August 12, 2018, https://www.dandodiary. com/2018/08/articles/securities-litigation/tesla-investors-file-securities-suits -elon-musks-take-private-tweets/.

16. Andy Hertzfeld, "Pirate Flag," Folklore, August 1983, https://www.folklore.org /StoryView.py?story=Pirate_Flag.txt.

17. Amy Fung, "Steve Jobs Getting Together A Players," YouTube video, October 18, 2013, https://www.youtube.com/watch?v=7yh7ikSQwKg.

18. Elon Musk holds similar beliefs about team meetings, advising his managers to get rid of large meetings altogether, and involve no more than four to six people when meetings are necessary. He also told Tesla employees they should leave a meeting when it is clear they are not adding value. See Catherine Clifford, "Elon Musk's 6 Productivity Rules, Including Walk Out of Meetings That Waste Your Time," CNBC, April 18, 2018; Alex Hern, "The Two-Pizza Rule and the Secret of Amazon's Success," *The Guardian*, April 24. 2018, https://www.theguardian.com /technology/2018/apr/24/the-two-pizza-rule-and-the-secret-of-amazons-success.

19. Chris O'Brien, "Steve Jobs' management legacy at Apple can be glimpsed in recently disclosed SEC letters," *VentureBeat*, October 6, 2015.

20. Timothy B. Lee, "How Apple Became the World's Most Valuable Company," *Vox*, September 9, 2015, https://www.vox.com/2014/11/17/18076360/apple.

21. "Arianna Huffington on the Culture at Uber," *Wall Street Journal*, October 23, 2017, https://www.wsj.com/articles/arianna-huffington-on-the-culture-at-uber -1508811600.

22. Ken Kocienda, *Creative Selection* (New York: St. Martin's Press, 2018), 13.

23. Jeffrey Pfeffer, "The Hidden Costs of Stressed-Out Workers," *Wall Street Journal*, February 28, 2019, https://www.wsj.com/articles/the-hidden-costs-of-stressed -out-workers-11551367913.

24. Parmy Olson, "BlackBerry's Famous Last Words at 2007 iPhone Launch: 'We'll Be Fine,'" *Forbes*, May 26, 2015, https://www.forbes.com/sites /parmyolson/2015/05/26/blackberry-iphone-book/#3bc0018363c9.

25. Jessi Hempel, "A Short History of Facebook's Privacy Gaffes," *Wired*, March 30, 2018, https://www.wired.com/story/facebook-a-history-of-mark-zuckerberg -apologizing/.

26. Mike Isaac and Daisuke Wakabayashi, "Russian Influence Reached 126 Million through Facebook Alone," *New York Times*, October 30, 2017, https://www .nytimes.com/2017/10/30/technology/facebook-google-russia.html.

27. David Meyer, "Deemed a 'Digital Gangster' by the U.K., Facebook Now Says It's 'Open to Meaningful Regulation,'" *Fortune*, February 18, 2019, https://fortune .com/2019/02/18/facebook-dcms-uk-report-digital-gangster/.

28. Walter Isaacson, "The Real Leadership Lessons of Steve Jobs," *Harvard Business Review*, April 2012, https://hbr.org/2012/04/the-real-leadership-lessons-of-steve -jobs.

29. Dennis K. Berman, "Arianna Huffington on the Culture at Uber," *Wall Street Journal*, October 23, 2017, https://www.wsj.com/articles/arianna-huffington-on -the-culture-at-uber-1508811600.

30. Walter Isaacson, "The Real Leadership Lessons of Steve Jobs," *Harvard Business Review*, April 2012, https://hbr.org/2012/04/the-real-leadership-lessons-of-steve -jobs.

31. Allen, *Idea Man*, 75.

32. Amy Edmondson, "Psychological Safety and Learning Behavior in Work Teams," *Administrative Science Quarterly* 44, no. 2. (June 1999): 350–83, http://www.jstor .org/stable/2666999.

33. The concept of a "double-bind" suggests that communication can contain two conflicting messages that are fundamentally at odds with each other. In the case of psychological safety, there is the risk that people are encouraged to be open and direct—but not so open and direct that they offend others and make them feel less safe.

34. Brandon Griggs, "10 Great Quotes from Steve Jobs," CNN Business, January 4, 2016, https://www.cnn.com/2012/10/04/tech/innovation/steve-jobs-quotes /index.html.

35. Isaacson, "Real Leadership Lessons."

36. Steve Jobs, Interview with Bob Cringley, "The Lost Interview," Readable, recorded in 1995, http://www.allreadable.com/031f1FIL.

37. Michael Moritz, "Silicon Valley Would Be Wise to Follow China's Lead," *Financial Times*, January 17, 2018, https://www.ft.com/content/42daca9e-facc -11e7-9bfc-052cbba03425.

38. A character in a Dave Eggers novel suggests, "We've become a nation of indoor cats. A nation of doubters, worriers, overthinkers," *A Hologram for the King* (New York: Vintage, 2013), 13.

39. Kayla Hinton, "Detroit; An Abandoned City?," *Spartan Newsroom*, July 12, 2017, https://news.jrn.msu.edu/2017/07/detroit-an-abandoned-city/.

40. Cheryl Howard, "Abandoned Detroit: Exploring the Largest Abandoned Site in the World," CherylHoward.com (blog), November 11, 2018, https://cherylhoward.com/packard-automotive-plant/. Other business operated in some of the plant buildings into the 1990s.

41. Mark J. Perry, "Animated chart of the day: Market shares of US auto sales, 1961 to 2018," American Enterprise Institute, June 28, 2019, https://www.aei.org /carpe-diem/animated-chart-of-the-day-market-shares-of-us-auto-sales-1961 -to-2016/.

42. GM, as did Ford and Chrysler, produced some regrettable cars in the 1970s, '80s and '90s—including the Chevrolet Vega, X-Cars, Chevrolet Chevette, and Saturns. See John Pearley Huffman, "10 Cars That Damaged GM's Reputation (with Video)," *Popular Mechanics*, November 24, 2008, https://www .popularmechanics.com/cars/a3762/4293188/. Huffman said of the Vega, "By the mid-1980s, Vegas were being junked so aggressively that some salvage yards in Southern California had signs up saying they wouldn't accept any more. When even the junkyard won't take a car, that's trouble."

43. Consider the functional backgrounds of the GM leaders just before and during the firm's decline in market share starting in the late 1960s and ending with its bankruptcy in 2009: James Roche (sales), Richard Gerstenberg (finance), Thomas Murphy (finance), Roger Smith (finance), Robert Stempel (engineering), and Rick Wagner (finance). Most of these leaders gained general management experience as they rose to higher-level positions within GM but, other than Stempel, they were not trained in product design, development, or manufacturing. Their obsession appears to have focused on making the numbers work. I suspect that Steve Jobs would have said they failed, at least in part, because they weren't in love with the product they were producing.

ACKNOWLEDGMENTS

This book draws on the work of researchers, journalists, bloggers, and authors, as well as the thinking of the leaders profiled. I focused, in part, on Bezos, Musk, Jobs, and Kalanick because of the wealth of material available in the public domain on each individual—providing a rich database on which to examine the promise and pitfalls of obsessive leadership. They are fascinating leaders and I have benefited from "spending time with them," writing about their ideas, achievements, and missteps.

As with my previous book *Extreme Teams*, I am grateful for the influence of Dennis N.T. Perkins—a wise mentor who introduced me to the field of entrepreneurial leadership. Thanks to Michael Chayes and Jeff Cohen for challenging my ideas, over many years and several books. Joe Bonito gave support in a myriad of ways, professionally and personally. Cedric Crocker was generous in offering insights into the dynamics of Silicon Valley. I also benefited from the feedback and encouragement provided by my wife, Jackie; my daughter, Gabrielle; and my brother, John. Each, in his or her own way, contributed along the way.

The contributions of the HarperCollins acquisitions and editorial staff were significant—in particular, Tim Burgard, Sara Kendrick, Amanda Bauch, and Jeff Farr provided helpful input and managed the important work needed to move the book forward. I also enjoyed working with Fauzia Burke, who provided savvy marketing guidance.

INDEX

INDEX

ABOUT THE AUTHOR

Robert Bruce Shaw assists business leaders in building organizations and teams capable of superior performance. His specialty is working closely with senior executives, as individuals and as groups, on organizational and leadership effectiveness. He has authored numerous books and articles including *Extreme Teams: Why Pixar, Netflix, Airbnb and Other Cutting-Edge Companies Succeed Where Most Fail*; *Leadership Blindspots: How Successful Leaders Identify and Overcome the Weaknesses that Matter*; and *Trust in the Balance: Building Successful Organizations on Results, Integrity, and Concern*. Robert holds a Ph.D. in Organizational Behavior from Yale University.